D1738545

The Countenance of the Father

ADRIENNE VON SPEYR

The Countenance
of the Father

Translated by
Dr. David Kipp

IGNATIUS PRESS   SAN FRANCISCO

Title of the German original:
Das Angesicht des Vaters
second edition, 1981
© 1955 Johannes Verlag, Einsiedeln

Cover art: *God Reprimanding Adam and Eve*
Monreale Cathedral, Italy.
Scala/Art Resource, New York

Cover design by Roxanne Mei Lum

© 1997 Ignatius Press, San Francisco
All rights reserved
ISBN 0-89870-620-3
Library of Congress catalogue number 96-78011
Printed in the United States of America ∞

CONTENTS

I

THE FATHER BEFORE CREATION

With the genesis of the world, the Father reveals himself as the Creator of all things; through his act of creation he manifests who he is. But he was present before creation, together with the Son and the Spirit in an essential unity. The fundamental attribute of the Father is his being a father: this is the primary thing the Son and the Spirit experience of him, just as it will be the first thing that men will know of him. Being a father implies, of course, a state of being antecedent. Those who recognize him as the Father thereby attest that he is their predecessor and that they come after him. They descend from him; he is the origin. This relation of origin and succession encompasses the whole being of the two related parties. If one considers the Son, one discovers this: it is his essential attribute to be a son; his whole frame of mind is like that of a son; each of his qualities characterizes him as the Son and thus also in his relatedness to the Father. Implicit here is not some obligation that has been externally imposed upon him but a right and a duty conferred upon him through his innermost being. And in order to evidence the Father, he does not ask the observer to look first at him, the Son, and then turn his gaze beyond, and away from, him in search of something else—but rather, he surrenders up himself, lays himself open, so as to reveal, through that very gesture, the Father.

The Father exists from eternity in concealment; but this concealment does not prejudice his fatherhood: it is mirrored forth in the Son and the Spirit, who reveal him as being the Father. When he eternally actualizes his fatherhood, forever generating the Son, forever effecting the Spirit's procession from the relation between Father and Son, it is through those acts that he is recognized as a father, is revealed with absolute clarity as a father. If we had insight into the divine processions, we would also see how alive the Father is in them, how fully they are a real happening within eternity—not mere static existence, mere omnipresence, but a process whose foundation is the Father. When one observes a person in prayer—his hands folded, his eyes closed, kneeling quite motionlessly—he seems to be inactive; nothing seems to be happening. But if one knows that he is praying, one can also know and experience him to be positing acts and effects that are the living proof of his faith and his being a Christian.

When we men attempt, in faith, to gain some sense of the Father, we must seek our means in the Son: the Son as visible in the New Covenant, the Son as linked to the Father and the Spirit in the Old Covenant; but also the Son as living together, before creation, with the Father and the Spirit in eternity. The creation of the world changed nothing in the Father's essence. He brought us into being and simultaneously revealed himself to us. But he was, from all eternity, always the one that he became, within time, for us: the bestower of being, the origin, who reveals himself in this gift. What he became for us, within time, he is for the Son eternally. If every origin is thus in him, it becomes clear to us that we can perceive nothing, believe nothing, love nothing, pass judgment on nothing, without coming back to him. The Son taught us to pray in this form: "Our Father". Those are his words, which reveal his position in relation to the Father and refer not only to a Father as he shows himself to us today, under the New Covenant, but to the Father as he is from eternity. Thus all our concepts must be related back to him if they are to take on their full meaning. Not just the concepts of faith or morality or some other specific area of knowledge, but all concepts whatsoever point back to the primal concept of the Father, to him whom the Son expresses as the eternal Word; and the Son is there in order to attest, with the whole of his eternal being, to the idea and reality of the Father.

Before the world existed, the Father was alone with the Son and the Spirit in an eternally blessed unity that corresponded to his essence and already contained all the relations to the Son and the Spirit that are appropriate to that essence. Those were relations of love; and this divine, eternal love was disturbed by nothing: every thought that expressed it was anchored from eternity in the Father, finding in him, not merely a meaning, but one that signified fulfillment and richness in every respect. And everything, heaven as the place of God, eternity as the lastingness of God, the relations of the Divine Persons to each other—everything had the magnitude of God the Father. Every sort of infinitude was at his disposal, so that God's love might never encounter any limits. All concepts had godly dimensions. God measured himself against himself, the Son, and the Spirit. And he allowed his thoughts to test themselves on eternity. The constraints of the world and of man, the bounds that are set by man's spirit and his soul, did not yet exist. So concepts arose from, and merged into, each other and supplemented one another in infinitude, in order to be worthy of the Father's greatness. If the Son will say of himself: "I am the way, and the truth, and the life", this does not mean that those three distinct attributes would, in eternity, blend into each other to the point of unrecognizability and therefore represent, even within time, only something blurred that would delineate the Son's essence indistinctly. Rather, each is a self-contained whole that does not encroach upon the others; they can merge with each other without losing their own identities. There is sufficient room in the Father, and he extends that same room to the Son and the Spirit, in whom everything that has a name can remain an unimpaired whole and can fulfill itself, beyond its relation to the Father, anew in both. That is why no concept needs to come to a halt, as if at a boundary, within the Son, being able to disclose a vista on the Father only from beyond that boundary; rather, a view of the Father is thrown open from within the Son, through his essence and mission. Whoever sees the Son sees the Father, because he explicates the concept and essence of the Father for us in such a manner that, through his words, which are the Father's words, the Father is revealed. And yet no one has seen the Father, unless it be the Son. In his inaccessible light and mystery (one might say in the modesty and discretion of his being a father) the person of the Father is distinct from the person of the Son. He generates the Son, whom he allows to become visible; but he himself remains—as if the ultimate surprise for the eternity to come—within the reserved mystery of his fatherhood, which is manifested only through his acts, just as an anonymous donor is identified solely through his donations. And yet again, the Father is not anonymous, because the Son is his Word, which perpetually describes him, and the Spirit is the relation of love, which perpetually refers to him. But this description and this reference are, for us, merely an exercise in eternal life. We are subject to limits that will fall away after death: redemption through the Son enables us to apprehend the dimensions of God, which will make his grace visible to us not merely in symbols but in its own essence.

For the Son and the Spirit, however, the Father was visible from eternity, not only in his effects, but in his being and essence: as father, procreator, creator, and ruler in all his magnificence. He was this in his timelessness, which lends its visage to any and every time, so that even the eternal time preceding creation is already stamped with the countenance of the Father and defined by it. The being of the Father with the Son and the Spirit is a fully determinate being, within which each Divine Person possesses his own countenance, even though it shows itself only within the mutuality of the one divine essence.

$\sim$

Since the Father is consubstantial with himself from all eternity, nothing of what is carried out by him, or the Son or the Spirit, or all three acting in common, and also nothing of what mankind, or some individual man, might undertake for or against him, can change him. He remains the one who he is, who foresees everything from eternity, who assumes responsibility for the whole future work of creation, including what will be effected in it by the Son and the Spirit. This responsibility remains in all respects a fatherly one: not only for what he, as the Father, will do, but also—as if involving a kind of supraresponsibility—for what the Son and the Spirit will do. This responsibility is active in him from eternity; it is part of his eternal life, and, since that life is love, part of his love. And inasmuch as he undertakes things from a position of direct or commissioned responsibility, the spirit of his love inheres in those undertakings; out of love, he creates new responsibility toward himself: which will therefore be authentic responsibility, that is, responsiveness to what he asks, and will contribute to the fullness of his work or indicate the fullness of his expectation.

And we undoubtedly gain our easiest access to the Father's essence through the words of the incarnate Son. But we must not overlook the fact that those statements, while made in the context of a certain historical period, have eternal validity. Not only are they just as relevant and vital today as they were when he uttered them, but even then they pointed toward the Father as he eternally is; the words of the Son have the power of expressing what is everlasting. And the Son speaks as the Word of the Father himself; we can thus make inferences from the words to their speaker, from what is stated to what is described, from the Son to the Father, from transient time to enduring eternity, and from the created world to God's heaven. And those inferences are not inherently self-limiting conclusions but always imply an openness: harboring the potential for new conclusions, other conclusions, divine conclusions, amounting in each case to a beginning, and thus being more like a key than a lock.

And when the Father sets about creating the world, he does so not only in mutual agreement with the Son and the Spirit but also in an essential interchange of love with them. The prominence of the Father in creation—who, as Creator, is accompanied by the Son (since the Father arranges everything with a view to the Son) and also by the Spirit (since, at the beginning, the Spirit moves over the face of the waters)—this prominence of the Father (in association with the Son and the Spirit) points ahead to the later prominence of the Son on the Cross, when the Son will commend his spirit into the hands of the Father. The Cross will be, in a sense, an echo of the creation of the world. In the desolation of the Son who hangs from the Cross and, at the point of death, consigns his spirit to the Father, the presence of the Father and of the Spirit is no less manifest than is, in the creation of the world by the Father, the presence of the Son (in view of whom everything is created) and of the Spirit (who moves over the waters). In this mutually reflective relationship between Cross and creation the unity of trinitarian activity is evidenced, so that—as we can infer from the Son's words to the Father—we too are able, in an analogous way, to move from the standpoint of creation toward the Father and his timelessness. (Of course the Son on the Cross is a man, whereas the Father in creation is solely God; but the Son is a *God*-man, and it is as *such* that he calls, in his desolation, to the Father. And insofar as the Father and the Spirit assist the *God*-man on the Cross, there is a genuine parallel between Cross and creation. And just as it is not possible to replace the suffering Son, on the Cross, with the Father or the Spirit, so, too, it is unacceptable to substitute the Son or the Spirit, in an equivalent sense, for the creating

Father.) In the Christian faith, it makes little difference —although the inherent directionality of time cannot be annulled—whether we reason back from the Cross to the prior being of the Father, or whether we choose to look ahead to the Cross from the viewpoint of that prior being. Creation's movement toward the Son, the Cross' return to the Father—both come together at any point within the triune, eternal God we attempt to grasp. And yet it is impossible, by such procedures, to draw a firm line within God, on the basis of which we could, with mathematical certainty, extrapolate other points and construct a geometrical figure. God and his plan for the cosmos cannot be represented in figures; we can never transfer ourselves to the locus of his essence, of his intentions, of his decisions. His love, his responsibility, and his essence always can ultimately be grasped only in faith, that is, in the faith entrusted to us—though it must be added that God, despite his immutability, can always alter, open, and expand anything that appears to us a closed matter. Concepts like the love, responsibility, or Word of the Father are certainly filled with a particular meaning for us, but that meaning can never be exhausted, because it remains (as conceptual) something creaturely even within faith. The distance between God and creatures is so great that we cannot, even in faith, bridge the gap by means of any concept. No more than we can define the Son as "he who lived among us as a man" can we exhaustively characterize the Father by stating, for instance, that he has existed from eternity. Statements are possible and pertinent, even to the point of appearing to satisfy our faith and our human understanding. In truth, however, God's real essence is infinitely greater than that which is "real" for us: in comparison to our reality, he is a transreality that surpasses us not only in scope but also in substance; and, indeed, surpasses our knowledge, belief, and intuition to an infinite degree in every respect. Our knowledge is fragmentary, so much so that we cannot even say that any single piece of it, at least, is adequate. We can no more describe God's essence than explain the mode of duration that preceded creation; we can attempt to string our units of time together— our days and nights and years—in unimaginably great quantities, yet we do not thereby generate a concept of eternity, not only because the greatest possible summation is insufficient, but even more because the units of time out of which we form that summation have no applicability to eternal duration. We can never say, even approximately, what a day like ours would mean in terms of God's proto-eternal day. When God brings the world and transient temporality into being, he has at his disposal the immensity and boundlessness of his own measure; and it is in pure grace and love that he presents us, from his inexhaustible storehouse, with a "something" that we can experience and measure and on the basis of which we are permitted to enter into relation with his own "something".

II

THE FATHER AND CREATION

Whoever lives in love, in a living, reciprocated love, also lives in joy. When the Father brings forth the world, he produces for himself something expressive of both: of his love and of his joy. He imparts order to chaos, and this bringing of order, this "purposeful arranging of things", is an expression of his joyous activity. He bestows on the world a share in his own heavenly order. To be sure, space and time, in their boundedness and temporality, imply a special creaturely order, one that is oriented toward man (to whom this world is to be given); but this act of ordering takes place with a view to an original order, which is that of the Father together with the Son and the Spirit. The world's order is an expression of the kingdom of heaven, an image of heavenly space, a correlative of heavenly time. The Spirit, who moves over the waters, bears witness to this relationship; and he attests to it, not like some passive observer reporting what he chances to see, but by giving a unified, enduring, and active testimony. For the Father, the Spirit is the eternal, living documentation of his eternal plan and its realization within time. But the world is created with a view to the Son, and his part, from the very first, is to receive it and take responsibility for it; the world's inherent directedness toward him is something that bears on him, from the outset, in the most active way—as if, on the day of creation, the Father had committed into the Son's hands, work by work and stone by stone, this gift of his love.

Just as a creative artist steps back in order to contemplate the completed form of the work that he had originally conceived, so, on the seventh day, the triune God rests and contemplates the completed work of creation. What was planned has become a reality, and the God in three Persons finds this reality good. This is a single common judgment, yet it is also internally differentiated in accordance with each Person's special qualities and relation to the world. In a certain sense, the Father has created the world as something separate from himself, which he positions at a distance before him; what has been thus placed is taken over by the Son so that it might be directed toward him and the Father's intent be realized, while the Spirit beholds from the outset, in this good situation, the sharing of all created things in the exchange of divine love. This goodness of creation has an expansive character: it is not a limited goodness, such as would correspond to some moral code or coherent point of view, but a goodness in God's sense. Creation is something worthy of God's love. It is intrinsically able to represent what God had resolved to achieve. It is capable of being taken over by the Son and of being animated by the Spirit. This capacity is one for correspondence within the responsibility of the Father, a responding of the world to the Creator, indeed, an embracing of the Father by the world. Latent in it is also the first word of affirmation by the first man to the Father and, implicitly, his still unconscious word of affirmation to the Son and the Spirit. When God comes to Adam in paradise, the latter stands before him in readiness to believe, receive, and acknowledge as his own whatever God reveals and presents to him and to accept as fitting what God requires of him.

Later, when the Son of man comes to perform his miracles, "a power" will "go forth from him": that activity will take its toll on him, will produce a certain exhaustion in him; he will put something into it that is part of his most personal being and life and that turns each miracle into another step toward the Cross. This is required by the order of the Incarnation. For the Creator, however, the creation of the world is in no way a weakening, exhausting activity. Inasmuch as God creates the world, he increases his kingdom. As the Father, he glorifies his relation to the Son and the Spirit, since, in this act of creating, he also establishes new relations to the world for the Son and the Spirit, which enable his fatherliness—in itself as well as for us—to radiate forth in a new, more profound light. The creation of the world is, for him, an expansion of his fatherly attribute, and yet—as accords with God's

essence—not at the expense of the other Persons, but
in such a way that the Son and the Spirit, and even
man, are included in the glorification.

If, in that imitation of Christ that is required of
man, the triune God demands devotion as an indivisi-
ble whole, if he places man from the very start under
the law of the "always-more" (which may seem to man
an excessive demand), then it is because the Father, already at the time of creation, has adhered to that law.
He created the world with a certain inherent quality of
always-more, insofar as it is intended to progress toward
the Son and to be taken up into the exchange of divine
love by the Spirit—something that not only arouses joy
in the three Persons but obligates them to show love
for all creatures; and this law of love finds its echo in
man. God has created a beautiful world; he has filled it
with countless things that—through their form, color,
sound, and sense—bring happiness to man, give depth
to his existence and direction to his outlook. But since
these things, in their beauty, subtlety, and fullness, are
all created with a view to the Son, and since the movement toward him is evident in man, the Father has,
from the very first, expanded the meaning of man's life
beyond the world and toward himself; he does not allow his Son's future brother to become wholly merged
with the limitedness of worldly things, to rest satisfied
at the level of finite beauty; rather, he guides him toward himself, refers him to the Son, describes to him
the nature of the Spirit. He sees that worldly things

themselves, in relationship to man, develop and endure in such a manner that they, too, in their own way, come to participate in the ever-expanding demand for devotion that is made on man.

As long as nothing finite had yet been created, God contemplated only himself—the Infinite. From the beginning of the existence of the created world, he has also allowed his gaze to rest on its finitude. That does not limit him; and yet he, as the one who eternally moves farther, now knows something like a halting at some specific point; and even when he looks out beyond that point, it is not thereby annulled in its finitude. The same thing holds true of time. And God brings both space and time into relationship not only with eternity but also with one another: the finite with the finite. The world is full of things that undergo change: what the morning witnesses is different in the evening; each coming day brings its new surprises. And the surprising is new beauty and new meaning. And when, at the end of each day of creation, the Father observes his work and judges it good, and the Son and the Spirit share in making that judgment, then this goodness of things has an inexhaustible meaning: it will propagate itself and continue on, both providing the surety and forming the matrix for the new. The diversity of relations that are constantly emerging has an unforeseeable quality: animals enter into new relations with plants, men with animals and plants and rocks and soil, and the tendency of each relation, whether at the generic or the individual level, is toward further goodness and richness.

Such fullness comes from God's heaven; but it is created with a view to the Son in heaven, toward whom the Father's fullness is directed—although, as it were, on a roundabout path through earth. This roundabout path, this new element, glorifies the triune God; yet it is, at the same time, entrusted to the superintendence of man. He is given the world in order to rule over it, and both his rule and his relationship with all other creatures, like that with God, are to be good —for all this goodness stems from God and is therefore inexhaustible in its fullness. Hence, the relationships of worldly things to each other, and of man to worldly things, can never be exhausted; moreover, they themselves constitute the ultimate fullness of the good, since all worldly fullness points back to God and finds its true fulfillment only in God's transworldly fullness. Nonetheless, the goodness of the world is adequate in itself, adapted to creatures and all their needs. Nothing was left inadequate, because God devotes equal care to each of his works and takes an equal responsibility for each. One can distinguish the various days and works of creation, but ultimately they are inseparable in the divine will.

From within eternity, God looks upon patterned and

articulated time. It is good, it has duration before him, nothing about it is inferior. It is just different from eternity, since it was made for man, who is different from God. It is adapted to him and placed at his disposal, in order to give him a sense of autonomous efficacy, to help him come to fulfillment. This different thing was, however, created by God out of joy; that, too, is implicit in the term "good". Just as he arranged the earth and the sea, the sunrise and the sunset, the rain and the night—precisely that arrangement is right, enriching, and joy-bringing, not only for man, but in the sight of the triune God. Through creation, God bestowed a gift on himself, inasmuch as he gave this work its place in the fruitfulness of his love. The eternal processes in God are not interrupted by the work of creation or forced into the background but are only confirmed and glorified anew. And when God ultimately goes walking through paradise, that is a confirmation of his joy and love. He enjoys spending time in this created place.

And he enjoys meeting with man—whom he created after his likeness—in this place. It is not demeaning for him to go visit man; the place to which he betakes himself is worthy of him. Not only in its attributes of space and time, but because of everything he finds there. Having created everything with a view to the Son, he already discerns in Adam a prefiguration of the coming Second Adam, sees him as the man of his selection, the chosen one of his love. Already, then, Adam reminds the Father of the Son, and the Father

feels, when he is with man, that he is near the Son;
something radiates from man that leads him directly
back to the Son. And similarly, in his conversation
with man, in the answers man gives to him, the Father
recognizes his own Spirit, whom he has conferred on
man. Thus God had, indeed, created something different, and yet something complete, a partner worthy
of himself. This whole partnership between the Father
and man is realized in terms of a movement toward the
Son and the Spirit. In it, man already has a participation
in the eternal. One would misunderstand man if one
were to regard him solely as the culmination of visible,
finite creation; or as part of that historical path that, as
a rational creature, he is able to traverse. He participates in the triune God, not merely as a creation of the
Father, or merely through the witness of the Spirit, but
through having been expressly created with a view to
the Son. His contours are prominently delimited so as
to allow his participation in the unlimited to become
perceptible. It is a delimitation that he was created on
the sixth day; a delimitation that his nature, his span
of existence, his mental and physical life are finite. But
these limits are intended to create room, an area of
unused space, and a starting point in the direction of
the Son, that is, as something open-ended. Man, as that
which he was meant in truth to be, is a being whose
structure makes him something different from God yet
one who remains, through that very structure, oriented
toward the Son of God and bound to him—the Son

who is himself God and who, as such, confirms the godly origins of man and the godliness of the act of creation. He comes from the hand of the Father and moves down the future toward the Son, who, in the fullness of time, will reach out to welcome him.

Thus the circle of divine love is expanded. The measured creature allows the immeasurable, eternal, and infinite to appear as all the more lovable and joyful. The Father, in his fatherliness, takes pleasure in that. In creation, he has a new sphere in which to proclaim his being the Father, a new responsibility, which is of course shared with the Son and the Spirit, yet is such as to be eminently his own. He created for himself the world that his fatherliness had longed for, so as to expand and communicate his fatherly qualities. And now, since no sin clouds this relationship, the first human couple look up to the Father without any sense of anxiety. The responsibility that the Father delegated by installing man as ruler is not something troubling to him but only a joyous activity within the context of an obedience conferred by the Father and co-fulfilled by man.

But scarcely has God articulated the goodness of the world, observed its full correspondence to his will, when man falls away from his proper relationship. He no longer wants to remain within it, no longer wants to obey. The fatherliness of the Father is not called into question by sin. He remains the Father of this creature. But new measures are now forced upon him. Adam has taken leave of God; he will, along with his descendants, have to seek the way back to God. In order that he be made conscious of his remoteness, he is driven out: this distancing serves to illustrate his disobedience. Man now stands in a different relation to God, but God remains the Father, and the interchange of eternal love endures in heaven. All of human life will henceforth be an unseeing quest for the lost homeland of love. Later, through the Son's path on earth, which originates from and returns to the Father, this blind seeking will be transformed into the possibility of finding. But there where the Son advances with clarity and fullness, the sinner just stumbles unknowingly and falteringly onward. What is imposed upon him is not primarily suffering but punishment; the suffering is borne, in its fullness, by the Son. That punishment includes, of course, various kinds of suffering, but only in an indirect form, since all human suffering is undergone in relation to the Son, as an unconscious participation in his Cross, an unrecognized tie to his still unforeseeable destiny. But the Father remains a father, and the punishment is a fatherly one. Man assumes the role of the lost son: it is just that he does not know this. He does not know the goal of his journey, and this forms the beginning of his punishment. He will also have to take upon himself the burdensomeness of work; his work will accompany his life and give shape to it to such an extent that one will be able to gauge from it the age and maturity of the man.

In creation, the Father, too, accomplished a "work",

performed an apparently concluded deed. For him, this work was a joy, and at the end he saw the outcome: that it was good. Man, by contrast, cannot assess the actual outcome. He sees merely that the freedom he has chosen transforms itself into a new prison, in which it is quite difficult to find God. The simplicity of life in paradise has vanished; he finds himself in a kind of tunnel where he has been deprived of vision. The bereftness of this has so punishing a character that man no longer understands the measures taken by the Father and can no longer maintain an undivided trustfulness toward him. His religious position has been thrown into utter disorder: through his own guilt, of course, but this condition of guilt has struck him blind. He is forced to go searching for what he had once possessed; but what he had possessed was the unquestioning nature of an existence in God, the childlike relationship with the Father, the profound knowledge that nothing but good can come to him from God. He can only go searching for this now, like someone who does not know the way, like someone carrying the load of time, burdened with a past; whereas formerly his past had been simultaneous with the present. In the presence of God, nothing of his former days was lost to him; they were days that, through their clarity and transparency, only intensified his pure relationship with the present God. Today, the past has been taken from him, and this loss is a torture to him. He remains caught up in an open question that he puts to God without being sure that he is really asking it; it is alive in him, but he experiences its aliveness only insofar as it tortures him; thus he stands in his own way.

And yet the Father remains. He must look on as his child torments himself and becomes alienated from him; but precisely because he is a father, he cannot just spontaneously intervene. Rather, he must leave mankind to the path of maturing experience, which it has already unknowingly chosen. From man's perspective, his fatherhood seems exhausted in standing by and watching, having taken on, in a way, the role of the Holy Spirit as witness. But in truth he is preparing to send the Son and the Spirit, precisely in confining his own intervention to the narrow history of the chosen people. Meanwhile, he leaves the rest of humanity with the feeling of its false sovereignty, which is burdened by the emancipation through sin and its consequences. These consequences extend to everything that constitutes man's life: his relationship to God, to his neighbor, and to all other creatures.

Man's dialogue with God has now assumed the form of "prayer". It is no longer simply a natural approach to God, the running of the newly arisen creature toward the arms of his Creator, but rather the considered, difficult, halting words of the sinner to his judge. And yet even in judgment, God remains the Father. It is just that the accused sinner can no longer see into the thoughts of the judge: his guilt curtails his vision and distracts him, it inclines him toward creating a different order from the one set up by God. What man would like most would be to leap free of his current relationship, position himself in a new place, and initiate from there a new relationship, devised by himself, to God. But he remains captivated by his old path, and his obsession with himself, his life, and its course causes that path to take ever more excessive and futile turns and detours. Were he to keep patiently to the path of punishment, then his expiation would undergo a change and also be shortened. But inasmuch as he goes on sinning, constantly devising new things that run counter to God's plan, he makes his path continually longer and less foreseeable. And if the Father is now to start issuing edicts, and raising his voice, and warning and punishing, the misunderstandings will multiply still further, since the sinner wants none of that and can no longer tolerate being on the path toward which God points him.

III

THE FATHER AND
THE OLD COVENANT

God the Father gave man the faith through which he can find his support, direction, and meaning in life. In order to possess all this, he need do nothing more than truly believe, that is, live in childlike dependence on the Father and trust in his help. God's fatherliness implies that he will not desert man, that he remains ready to help him bear the responsibility for his existence and to grant him, whenever necessary, signs of his presence. And that is particularly necessary whenever man falls into sin and must be brought back again.

God makes use of the most diverse means understandable to man in order to proclaim his presence to him. He sends constantly new directives and signs to his chosen people, and the instances of both point, through the explicit words, beyond themselves to new revelations that can be expected. Thus, already in the Old Covenant, the faith that has been given to man is capable of any amount of expansion and can, through the new content that it acquires, not just consolidate but also propagate itself, inasmuch as it takes on apostolic force. But men go on sinning, and it is as if the Father's revelatory grace were engaged in a competition

with sin. The turning away of man and his reclamation
by God both intensify. The process of divine choosing is meant to subserve this revelation. God selects
particular individuals, who then stand in sharp contrast
to those who have not been chosen. A most striking
instance of this occurs right at the beginning: Abel's
sacrifice is accepted, while Cain's sacrifice is rejected.
At the time, even those making the sacrifices are themselves unable to solve the riddle behind this choice;
they unravel it only subsequently, through their lives,
which bring to light their respective inner dispositions.
But in this choosing and not choosing, as in reward-
ing and punishing, God always remains the Father. Not
through intervening with excessive haste, but always,
so to speak, following after, inasmuch as he interprets,
affirms, or rejects what has occurred.

A seeming contradiction runs through this portrayal
of God: the same Creator who presented himself originally as the loving Father and kept company with Adam
in paradise has now taken on the countenance of a judge
and often, indeed, of one enraged. Man is supposed to
worship him, to offer sacrifices to him, and to seek
him with all his heart; he is supposed to construct,
out of the elements of his faith and the guidelines that
have been issued for his life, a kind of church of the
Old Covenant. He experiences this as a contradiction.
But the contradiction lies in him; like a blind man he
runs constantly up against the presence of grace, which
he nevertheless cannot correctly receive: his eyes are

veiled, and it accords with this condition that the Father has not yet disclosed the existence of the Son and the Spirit. The mystery of triune love has still not been made evident. God's word points in its direction, but the full sense of that word is still sealed for the believer. Hence, his concept of God remains divided. From his own life he sees that, when he is just and believing, God takes a fatherly attitude toward him, promising and conferring things that enable him to exist in grace and joy. But he also sees that other men have things far less easy than he, that the ways of fatherly justice remain impenetrable even to the believer. Sin, as a world of its own filled with its own questions and problems, imposes itself in a divisive and obscuring manner between himself and God, so powerfully that many among the people perceive that they will never rid themselves of this obstacle by their own efforts.

God gave the people the law. But to keep completely to the law is so difficult for man that, in its presence, he feels the sense of contradiction in his heart grow deeper, and an obstinacy begins to well up within him. He begins to behave like a child who cannot bear the sight of his father, shuts himself up in his own way of thinking, and refuses to acknowledge the father's measures, reprimands, and punishments. Thus the gap between the world of the Father and the world of sinners widens, and it begins to seem as if God's fatherhood will never suffice to bridge that gap again. But the solution will not come through the Father's giving up and sending the Son in his place. Rather, the Father will reveal himself not merely as the Father of man but, more profoundly, as the Father of the eternal Son; and God's fatherhood will thus provide the unifying span between those two so infinitely different relationships: to the most unjust of men, and to the supremely just, complete God. And while he must punish man and confront him with riddles and restrict him through laws, he thinks constantly of the love and the freedom of the Son. In one of the Father's thoughts, there must be room not only for the darkest of sinners but also for the supremely bright Son—enough room to allow him to regard both the Son's being and man's being from the one, undifferentiated viewpoint of divine justice. This fatherhood in relation to the only begotten, eternal Son is still kept hidden; the time is not yet ripe for sending out the Son, for proclaiming him in such a way that believers will recognize him as their brother, who, by virtue of his perfection, enjoys the privileged status that is the essence of all chosenness. On the other hand, God cannot allow even the worst of sinners to fall; for he is a man, and the Son, too, is to become a man. He cannot render the Incarnation of his Son impossible in advance through that one sinner, nor can he repudiate, through that sinner, his own creation. Everything must, with a view to the Son, be kept open and hanging in the balance.

Thus one can sense in advance the form that the Father's justice will take. In order to protect the human race, to which his Son will belong, he must show it his severity and not just his mildness, in fact, his righteousness before his love, the latter of which still remains so hidden that its existence can become questionable to sinners. But that very law that irritates them, and which they find burdensome and incomprehensible, will reveal to the Son the Father's love; it will suit him to perfection and pose no difficulties at all. Everything turns on this difference between heavy and light, between being unable to obey because of ultimate weakness and obeying as a matter of course, between the concealing and the demonstrating of love, between the reserved and the expressed word.

~

It is not easy to describe the way in which God regards man under the Old Covenant. He sees in him the creature he has formed; but he sees his spirit tied down to sin, which is a powerful reality; at the same time, man is caught up—by virtue of faith and promise— in a countermovement, through which he attempts to find God and his Holy Spirit once again: God the Creator and that Spirit who moves over the waters, who is ready to impart and sacrifice himself and to complete the Father's work. Sin was directed against this Holy Spirit; it deprived man of his participatory place in the divine, which the Father held ready for him within the Spirit. Faith and sin are both on the move, and man is the battlefield for both. And now it looks as if man must always first stumble over sin before he can find the Holy Spirit, as if the guilty one must always first run up against himself as an obstacle before, having overcome this, he can embrace faith and be taken into possession by it. Under the Old Covenant, God's Spirit stands as if in chains: deprived of his ultimate potential for giving himself to man, of his strongest power to turn man toward the Father. He holds his gift ready, in joyous anticipation of presenting it, but the one for whom it is intended is half turned away from him. And so the Spirit, who is a Spirit of turning toward, is unable to communicate himself fully to him. But it is part of the Father's justice that he must search within man for the presence and work of the divine Spirit and, in fact, must judge man according to his possession of spirit. This is required by the Spirit's original participation in the work of creation, and the Father cannot tolerate the prospect that man might drive God's Spirit out of creation. Through all time the Spirit proceeds from the Father and the Son; he is always found to be manifest in the Holy Trinity. But since the inception of the world, he wishes to live in, and blow through, the Father's work as well; and so it is necessary that the Father find him not only in his original state of presence in God but also in his effects on the world (which man only hinders). The Father also owes it to the Spirit to take care that the latter's divine love should not go to waste in the world. That is why he keeps the Spirit, who cannot live in sinners, temporarily hidden.

Prior to sin, the Father was present, by his will, on earth as well as in heaven; and this unity of his presence took place through the descent of his Spirit of love into the world. After the arising of sin, man's guilt led to an interruption of the exchange of love between God and the world. In heaven, the interchange continues on; there, everything remains in its unshakable, eternal place. Man, however, having been deprived of God's Spirit, has lost his true place, his certainty, his measure; his distancing from God is characterized by the non-measure and the non-spirit of sin, and man would have to fall into an abyss, into nothingness, to seek refuge in sheer flight, if the Father did not, through his punitive justice, uphold at least one relationship, which manifests itself in man as a thirst for the lost goods of the Spirit. Adam ate the forbidden fruit; in so doing, he not only performed an act of disobedience but also put into his mouth a taste that was not intended for him by God: the taste of what is distant from God, of life without God's Spirit, of existing in mere transience. Such an existence should not be to his taste. His relation to the things of this world, over which he should have dominion, was meant to be a life in the order and the Spirit of God. Now, instead of that, the measureless, the unordered, has come between God and man, and man's most fundamental standpoint —his self-orientation, his duration, his magnitude—

has thereby become questionable. In place of the cosmos of the Spirit man has introduced the chaos of sin. It is no longer the neutral chaos that God, in the beginning, had divided into regions and times and distances and orders through his act of creation; it is something without rules, which stands opposed to God's infinitude, almost as if man had devised an adequate weapon with which to counter God. And thus the Father must, in the Old Covenant, impose wholly new measures upon his disobedient child in order that he be humbled nonetheless: through suffering and anxiety and hopelessness. And those measures should be so thoroughgoing that the one humbled might not be threatened, in his new life, by a new onslaught of chaos, that is, that the same thing might not happen once again to the Son, in his redemptive work, that happened to the Father in the context of creation.

IV

THE FATHER AND THE PROPHETS

God shows himself to man as the Father by allowing man, his creature, to participate in his divine life while, at the same time, offering him the possibility, through the living relationship between God and man, of living his worldly existence in a fulfilled way. This is an existence oriented toward God, a life of becoming that accords with the nature of his creaturely being. Inasmuch as man acquires a better knowledge of God in his triune revelation, he also penetrates more deeply into the Father's intentions for him, into the possibilities of his own life before the Creator. Man's turning away from God disrupts this development at its innermost level, since God must now conceal himself and, as a just judge, must effect punishment and expiation in order to show man his sins and their results.

Under the Old Covenant, the believer knows about mankind's primal history, the expulsion from paradise, and the choosing of Abel and the rejection of Cain, which initiates the long succession of choosings and rejections in the history of the Covenant. The Father likes to break through the laws of the world in certain ways, in order to stand suddenly before startled mankind as the living Lord over all laws: through demonstrations of power, decrees, and events that erupt unexpectedly and reveal God's presence. It is the presence of the sovereign Master, to whose law unruly man cannot but submit because it far outstrips all his own devices.

Interacting with this Lord of the Covenant seems to impart a special quality to Old Testament man's form of time. He lives in a reality that is always of today, in the midst of present actions and intentions; but his today is wholly determined, on the one hand, by the past history of the Covenant and, on the other, by that future toward which, on the basis of God's promises, the people moves. The God of righteousness, the God of man's ancestors, deigns to disclose to men of today a truth about the future, whose fulfillment is, in faith, certain. This Old Testament man—who as yet has scarcely any notion of what eternal life is, who is still so caught up in the reality of sin that his freedom of thought is confined largely to the present—experiences the opening of a doorway before him into what is coming, into the world as a totality, and from there into eternity. The man of today is promised things that God will realize, perhaps in later epochs, for his descendants. This promise ties man inextricably to the future; he understands that his knowledge of God's intent is not accidental: he is connected just as closely with that intent as with its coming fulfillment. He is part of the course of events that God projects into the future. If, however, God promises something today that he will unfailingly fulfill, then this demonstrates with certainty that, in God, both intent and realization exist in a superior, trans-enduring form of time, and that this trans-enduring world of God's has been disclosed, through the words that he has addressed to the people, within man's transient form of time. And it is not just through the content of these words that listening man comes to share in God's transcendent world but also through the forms that God selects when communicating them.

God makes use of voices and words, and he chooses men who are able to perceive those voices and words: men whose relationship to God is so living that it becomes a sensible reality, that they regard themselves not only as sinners and remote from God but as those who experience God's presence and receive his promise in words. They are the Lord's chosen ones; but they must be able to show responsibility for this chosenness before their fellow men, allowing what has been entrusted to them to become a living reality for others by communicating what they have received and imparting to others, with as much clarity as possible, some idea of the obedience through which they themselves are tied to God, so as to educate them toward a similar obedience. This gives them a privileged position among men as well, a distinction brought about solely by the presence of God that is granted to them. It is not something that man draws out of himself, confers on himself, or could obligate himself to by his own powers; it is God's irruption into this life, which brings consequences observable to all. Here, God appears to follow a certain method: he lets some things be proclaimed that can be confirmed in the shortest space of time and others that carry over into the distant future, with examples of each sort being presented in inextricable combination, so that the fulfillment of the first sort enables men to infer both the truth of the second and the authenticity of the prophet's mission.

The Son and the Spirit also participate in this prophetic revelation of the Father. The Son is to be found primarily in the content of the promises: he will one day bring them all to fulfillment. Already now, they are filled with his later coming, and whoever has ears to hear perceives in them already the first sounds of the good news. The Spirit reveals himself by transporting the prophet into a spiritual state that is alien to him as man, a sinner, and a descendant of the one who was driven out of paradise. He becomes intoxicated with the Holy Spirit; he experiences and testifies to things that he could never experience as a mere man; that are transmitted, disclosed, and explained to him by another; and that all have their locus within the perduring presence of God. Thus God reveals himself on two levels: in the content of the words that are heard, which is fulfilled in good time, and in the man who proclaims them, including his evident personal posture. This posture, as something newly arising, adapted to the Spirit and full of God's word, is a kind of after-sketch of the initial creation of man. Those who were everyday men suddenly become marked with a quality that they are perhaps not even capable of recognizing, because they would prefer not to acknowledge the change that the word has produced in them. Others recognize it even from a distance. For God not only entrusts his chosen ones with his mysteries but imbues them with something of his holiness. They are granted participation in things that no one can bear unless he is led, in strict obedience, by God. They have relinquished all making of personal plans; they are guided beings, who, in faith, proclaim and order what they do not fully grasp. No external power, no goal-oriented striving, nothing acquired by learning is capable of transforming a man as does the experienced word of God, when the Spirit gives triune testimony to that which the Father creates and orders and anchors in the Son. Thus the prophet becomes, through the Spirit that dwells within him, himself a testifier. He proclaims things about events and realities that have present truth only within God's trans-temporality. And that which he, as a prophet, stammers out, or perhaps proclaims with a firm voice and unbending stance, is something that he does not, in the end, himself understand, because it remains purely received, divine property.

In each of his words, however, God remains the Father; he bends down to his child in loving concern, in the steadfastness of a leader and guide. The child assesses how high above himself the Father stands, but he also feels how securely he is contained within the

resolute intent of God. He is directed, educated, pun-
ished and rewarded, given duties, helped through difficult times; he must suffer without understanding why,
yet is conscious, in the midst of this noncomprehen-
sion, of the Father's presence. And if the prophet must
also proclaim terrible things, he remains aware that, in
God, everything is right as it is. He cannot keep silent
about the truth, even if he might first wish to resist
it, because God, who guides him, is greater than his
thoughts, his will, or even his own needs. God's needs
outweigh any of man's needs. It is as one who has been
laid low by God's might that the prophet makes his
proclamations. Yet at the same time it is as one who
has been set on his feet and is allowed to look up to
his Father. Under the Old Covenant, the veiling of the
Father at the Cross is prefigured in the dark destinies,
and the incomprehension, hesitancy, and rebellion, of
the prophets.

~

The prophet, who becomes conscious of God immediately and personally, understands that this experience
may well remain one of faith but that its content is
an immense, divine world. As a believer, he knew of
its existence previously in the way that one knows,
through descriptions, some distant land; now he is in-
vited to step into this world. He hears God's voice, and
now he has an ear with which to make sense of it, an

organ never used before today, which now reveals its existence and capability. That dull confinement within the world, through which he was linked to other men, has been suspended; he has stepped out into the world of God, with senses that can apprehend it. If he previously had occasion to speak of other prophets' experience of God, he thus knew that such a thing existed; it was evidence for him of the ever-greater nature of God, of the respect that is required before him. But he knew this only in a theoretical way; and perhaps he had the feeling that he himself would never progress any farther in faith. Although his faith seemed something immediate to him, all its contents appeared mediated; his human task seemed to remain a nameless one, with God demanding of him the same sort of prayer and work that was expected of the rest of the people. Now he finds himself, in his entire being, suddenly transported into a new kind of existence. And when he apprehends God's voice, the meaning of the name "Father" opens itself to him as if for the first time. His respect before God is no longer this general—in a way shy—attitude of reserve; it is now the living fear and love of one who has been concretely addressed, who stands before his divine Father; the infinite difference between God and man is not erased but so transformed, through God's word, as to become the distance between a father and child.

And when the Father bridges the gap through his words and makes himself understandable to the prophet, this calls for a response from him that cannot come merely from the lips but demands the commitment of his whole personality; so that he must now summon up something that had been unsuspectedly latent within himself and put it into his answer. Through the demand thus placed on his whole being, through his having been called and installed in service, he gains a new recognition not only of himself but also of God's essence. For this sharing in God's world by apprehending his voice, this being permitted to respond out of an unsuspected depth—even if the response appears to him much too weak—shatters what he knew as the limits of his creatureliness. But precisely through being confronted with the limitlessness of God's fatherhood, as revealed in his voice, the prophet begins to sense what God had actually intended with his creature, what he had planned for and expected of him. God asserts this expectation in a new way by revealing it; he grants the prophet an insight that nevertheless still remains in God's keeping. The time of its being revealed through the Son, who will speak in human language, has still not arrived. Whatever comes from the sphere of the Father retains the strictness and weight of a justice that is incomprehensible to creatures. But the demand made upon man is so strict that he can respond to it only through something that resembles love, if it is not, in fact, love itself.

There is much fear in the lives of the prophets and much anxiety in their responses. Much that is terrible is also contained in the words that they must proclaim, words of threat and calls for repentance—as if justice were something that could not take its course apart from what induced fear. And when the prophet obeys the word and performs things that are understandable (even to himself) only in the context of this obedience to God, he does so as someone weakened, dazzled, and reeling. At most, he can seek consolation in God's words of promise: that another will complete and perfect what he himself ineptly foreshadows. And this hope is directed toward a future so incalculable that his present remains one of fear, that he carries out in fear what God demands, not with the confidence of a Christian, but with the trembling that accompanies a prophet's mission.

And yet he can gauge, on the basis of his experience of human fatherhood, how much of the fatherly exists in the God of the prophetic word. He feels himself in a position like that of a boy standing before his father: he listens attentively to what the Father says, and understands it up to a certain point, but the wider context and motives of the Father's actions remain veiled to him. He looks with reverence upon the Father's works and longs to comprehend something of them; he attempts, with tripping little steps, to keep pace with the Father's large, measured strides. He is proud whenever asked to lend a hand in some small way—anxious and proud at the same time, because God the Father remembered him and can use him for some task, however small.

And inasmuch as he performs his service by transmitting God's voice at the human level, the essence of man and creation is thereby disclosed to him in a new way; man has not, despite all his sin and deafness, lost the capacity—at the moment when God needs him and unlocks his hearing—to sense God's word. This is a hearing of overflowing fullness, which may seem, at the same time, deficient (since he does not understand everything); yet it is still clear enough to produce correct obedience through a response that is more than a vague approximation, clear enough to precipitate events that demonstrate the truth of the word and to subjugate the prophet—half-willingly, half-hesitantly—to the power of the Holy Spirit. He follows an infinitely superior being; he follows without fully comprehending, and yet he follows. He follows in an obedience that breaks his life to pieces and then puts it back together according to a plan incomprehensible to him, so that he might, in the future, have credibility before the people as a man of God. He is dispossessed of his own self, because God has drawn him so closely into the sphere of his will that he performs, out of this fatherly will, whatever is required of him.

Even if the prophet is often taken into service by God and must utter highly enigmatic truths and perform humanly incomprehensible things, he can still never boast of having a closeness to God that would allow him to rise, for once and for all, above darkness and adversity. As the Father, God speaks a language that cannot become fully intelligible to man. And since the expulsion from paradise, man, as a believer, cannot feel at home in God's domain or with God's use of words. He is a foreigner who can acquire a few fragments of the language, while at the same time knowing that, when God initiates his processes of judgment and places even the righteous on the scales of his justice, he will never comprehend the inner laws of that justice. And yet God allows him the sense of a certain continual advance, of a kind such as will no longer be possible under the New Covenant, when the entire sphere of seeing, hearing, and responding will be transformed through the love of the incarnate Son. Then the Son on the Cross will have been committed into the uttermost weakness of death, beyond which it is impossible to go still farther. God will then have shown and bestowed so much that the Christian will never stand anywhere other than at the beginning of fullness. Christians might envy Jews their possibility of "continual advance", but only because, in the Old Covenant, the fullness of the Son had not yet appeared.

V

THE FATHER SENDS THE SON

When reflecting on triune love as the basic characteristic of the divine essence, we attempt to form a conception for ourselves by starting out from certain concrete images of what we understand by "love". But if we remind ourselves that God's love is at the source of everything, that God's every word, his every revelation and action, already both presuppose it and refer back to it, then our notion threatens to flow out in all directions to such an extent that we are left with nothing definite at all. Love is now everywhere and in everything, and we end up clinging, discouraged, to the mere word and saying: It is simply all love; it encompasses everything, everything arises from it, and everything returns to it.

But if we try approaching this from the direction of the idea of the Father, the danger that our concept will become too general and empty can be minimized. The Father sends the Son, and that sending is an expression of fatherly love. And it is out of love that the Son allows himself to be sent. If a human father sets his son some task that he has himself conceived, one where he knows what steps to take to accomplish it, and whose results he can foresee, he thereby gives his son an opportunity to grow, to prove himself. To accomplish things that the father must recognize and praise. The initiative stems from the father, and he is also the reaper, who has followed the whole process and can evaluate things by the proper standards.

As long as the Father in heaven was merely the Father of the eternal Son, his fatherhood was purely a bringer of joy to him, since he experienced nothing from the Son but love. The movement through which the Son, as the ever-generated one, is returned to the ever-awaiting Father is a movement of eternal love. A spontaneous, unproblematic movement that includes the Spirit, is testified to by the Spirit, and is lent a form appropriate to his love by the Spirit. In this movement no obstacle, no contradiction is possible. The love is one of being as well as of doing, and its experience remains, within the triune reality, completely divine in every respect.

Once, however, the world has been created and men have sinned, the Father's love for his creatures no longer receives a response; every instance of rejection, half-heartedness, or forgetting is an affront to him, which he does not just register in a kind of elevated indifference but takes very much to heart. Every No from his creature affects him in his innermost truth and love. He does not just "act" offended; he *is* offended and *becomes* so in repeated new ways. Thus he needs to impose punishment; yet his punishments do not eliminate sin, for there always remains the possibility of saying No again and again.

So the triune God determines to send the Son. With this step, a new starting point is established, which is an act of free grace and can in no way be explained as following necessarily from certain premises. The Son is prepared, through Incarnation and redemption, to bring such a superabundance of love into the world that love will, in principle, outdo the power of sin. The omniscient Father knows the nature of the task that the Son thereby assumes and also that no one Divine Person can assume such responsibility without the others bearing their share as well. This accords with the impetus of divine love, which never withdraws, shows itself equal to every task required of love, and never takes anything from the treasure chest of love that could diminish it but only that which, through its radiance, will allow the common triune love to shine forth more brightly.

On the other hand, by sending the Son, the Father wants to confer new rights upon man, to provide him with a new certificate of whose child he is. The inconceivable is to be realized: that God the Father should be the Father not only of the eternal Son but also of sinful man. Previously, these two relationships were coexistent but unconnected. Were one to compare the assertions made by the eternal Son about his Father with those made by men about the Creator, the gap between the two would become glaringly obvious. The image that men construct consists—no matter how hard they try to avoid this—of nothing but human characteristics;

the concepts they employ either are not sufficiently broadened or have already become blunted. Someone lacking discernment would have to ask himself whether these concepts can really apply to the same God as that of the Son. But now, through the Incarnation, the Father wants to extend something of the eternal sonship to man as well. Therefore the Son is to become man, but without ceasing to be God; he unites in himself, in something like translated form, the two images of the Father—he, the one who unites both natures, without diminishment, in his Person. This Person will live among us and fulfill a mission that is divine but carried out in human flesh. Through this emergence of the Son and its associated revelation, the countenance of the Father takes on increased depth for men in an unexpected way. Now the statements of the eternal Son can also be understood and applied by them; indeed, they are enabled, in faith, to share in the vision that the Son receives from the Father. The Son, who lives as a man among men, has set himself the goal of bringing them closer to the Father; in this, he sees the fulfillment of his teaching and, at the same time, the culmination of his redemption. What he will achieve and suffer along the way remains a mystery of his most personal love, which always relates back to his having been sent by the Father; for there is no moment at which the Son views his mission as something detached, as belonging to him alone. He remains in the situation of one who carries out a commission that he accepts continuously, within a living interrelationship, from the commissioner.

Creation's inherent directedness toward the Son is now actively taken over by the Son, who, in the midst of the world as it is, among the men of his time, invests creation with a new directedness toward the Father. This act of taking over comes about through the Incarnation. The Father demonstrates his love for the Son inasmuch as he sends precisely him, whose own greatest wish is thereby fulfilled. At the same time, however, he demonstrates his love, as the Creator, for his creatures, inasmuch as he gives them his Son to be their brother and allows him to assume fleshly form by being born of a virgin through the Holy Spirit, thus finding a human womb to be worthy of carrying God. In that way, the Father evidences the degree of holiness that a creature is capable of through grace: not only does he entrust him with his most dearly beloved, but this creature even makes earthly life possible for a God-man. For God, human nature has not been so corrupted by sin that the Son could not carry out his mission as a man among men. It is not through the Son's presence on earth that the Father's relationship with the world first becomes a new one but already through the very resolution to send him into the world. He wishes to present man with a tangible proof of his love and thereby destroy any suspicion that the Creator had abandoned his creature.

∼

There was a time when God's eye had come to rest heavily upon Cain. Cain felt that God was looking at him; he felt the weight of the divine gaze, which he could not escape and could not forget. A dead-straight line ran from God's eye to Cain's eye, and the meaning of that line was judgment.

When God resolves to send his Son, the latter knows that the Father's eye will accompany him along his path on earth, while he will keep his own inner eye constantly directed toward the Father; and the meaning of this line between them will be love, an exchange of giving. God on earth will live and act in the presence of God in heaven, and the Father's eye will be a consolation and a stimulus to the Son. And the Son's mission will be formed entirely out of divine material, interwoven with all the Father's love of the Son and of creatures, and the Father will henceforth encompass both Son and creature in a single loving gaze. This look, this certification of everlasting presence, will serve the Son as a guideline for his performance of the Father's will; it will reveal to the Father where the Son is heading, and the Spirit will bear witness to their mutual look, both to all that this look definitely is *not*: there is no reciprocal desire to monitor, assess, demarcate, or support; and to what it really *is*: the clearly evident expression of an unsurpassable love.

Under the Old Covenant, the prophets anticipated, in their visionary state and for a brief time, something of the attitude of the Son and also themselves lived through, to a certain degree, something of the mode of existence of the Son, who knows that the Father's gaze rests upon him. Their experience pointed ahead to the New Covenant and not back, for instance, to the guilt-laden feeling of being seen that occurred with Cain. The same eye of the Father signifies punishment for Cain and grace for the Son. The same gaze brings both judgment and redemption, not just because everything is one in God, but because both Cain (who represents Adam here) and Christ need to be conscious of their being human. Beneath this gaze, both must come to experience what being human means for the Creator and Father: being human from the standpoint of creation and becoming newly human from the standpoint of Christ.

"He who formed the eye, does he not see?" God's seeing, hearing, and speaking, which are certainly attributed to him in an analogical sense, are still, in their bearing on the structure of man's being with its senses and faculties, so real, so concrete, that they cannot be replaced by any other terms of expression. The reality of the relation moves from eye to eye, from mouth to ear, even if it can never be reduced to statements in sensory terms. This relation is the evidencing of the Father's love for his creatures and, at the same time, an evidencing of the relationship of the generating Father to his eternal Son—whom he allows to become man in order that man might be allowed to experience love in a new way, in an experience so all-encompassing as to make the Father's gaze equally fundamental to the Cain who flees before him, to the Son who moves toward him, and even to the Son who feels himself abandoned on the Cross.

∼

When the Father sends the prophets, he issues them more or less short-term commissions. Their task is to proclaim certain of God's promises, including the punishments that God will inflict if man does not believe, does not obey. Along with this, the prophet can be equipped with spiritual power and a comprehensive view of a certain area of history. But it can also be the case that he gropes along in utter darkness and must entrust himself blindly to God's guidance. All of the individual prophetic destinies and situations are taken over by the Son and integrated into one encompassing and conclusive relationship. He knows the Father's will in its entirety. And yet he allows himself to be sent, that is, to be placed in the position of the prophets, in order, like them, to accomplish the Father's will on earth through concrete deeds. In this way, he transfers his eternal filial love—which always does what is of the Father and reigns in the kingdom of the Father—from heaven into the world of men. In addition, he takes over the strictest form of obedience to God that had previously existed, that of the prophets, in order to bring it to fulfillment. In fact, he follows it all the way back to the first Adam, so as to reclaim him, too, and lead him to the fullness implicit in the new mission of the Second Adam, with its broad spanning of the whole world, eternal time, and a clear view of the Father's will. The Son does not find this new order of things already there; he must create it through his own existence, through persevering in such a way, beneath the Father's gaze and within his will, that, through him, the Father becomes transparent: no longer partially and for individuals, as in the Old Covenant, but wholly and for all.

At the time of paradise, only a single human couple was present in one specific place on earth; God could keep company with no one else. At the time of the Son's mission, the world is full of men, and the Son, based in his own small part of the earth, has to proclaim the teachings of the Father in such a way that the whole world is addressed and gripped, that a movement of the whole toward the Father is initiated, and that the Son becomes the Master for the countless many. And these countless many no longer live, like Adam, in company with God; they live in forgetfulness of God, in a state of actual sin, often without realizing what they are doing and without being at all aware of the Son's existence among them. Through that existence, however, the Son introduces a factual element into the world that cannot be reversed. Through him, the relationship of the Father to creatures is altogether changed.

He is God and man; and no matter what he does in his human nature, he does it as a Divine Person. Thus the supernatural is dominant in him. For Adam in paradise, an innocent nature was dominant, and its relation to grace was simple and raised no questions. For the prophets, what dominates is a conflict between their nature and the supernatural that takes possession of it: they are pulled back and forth between the powerlessness of nature and the claim of the supernatural. For the Son, there is no longer any conflict, because he lives in the supernatural—which, as God, he himself is —and because his humanity is underpinned by his divinity. Thus his human nature can become an expression of his divine being. What he asserts humanly on earth is divinely true in heaven. This does not prevent his really being a man like all others, subject externally to the same limitations, feeling the same burdens and sorrows. He can, of course, should he choose to perform a miracle, make those limitations vanish; but in the everyday life in which he grows up, works, acts, and teaches, he is simply a man. When the eyes of his fellow men turn toward him, they at first see nothing but the man, just as his eyes see in them his fellow men. But the Son is, at the same time, God; and everything limited about him is a pathway and portal to the unlimited. And so the Son's view is expanded: he who was present at the creation of the world, he in relation to whom this world was created, well knows what the Father had wanted for men; hence, he discerns the

Father's will and intent in them even now. Men's sinfulness and turning away in no way obscure his view of the beginning, which makes him all the more able to appreciate the total injustice that man does to his Father. Everything that is of the Father and that affects man is present to him; he sees through man and beyond to the Father's will, to his plan for creation, to what he has now commissioned.

By virtue of this life in the sphere of the supernatural, the Son has a comprehensive view of his mission and the freedom to act at his own sovereign discretion within it—as opposed to the prophets, who found themselves subject to a rigid, servile obedience. In him, this freedom is just as full and autonomous as is his obedience to the Father. This holds true even regarding the prayer on the Mount of Olives, which, amidst all the anxiety, is still the free, spontaneous prayer of the eternal Son to the Father. The heavenly world of prayer in which he constantly lives, the vision of the Father, the unending pure accomplishment of the Father's will: all this, which both is open toward eternity and participates in it, is an essential part of his mission. His "reckoning" as a man proves to be in constant accord with the "reckoning" of the Father. Like a child, he has an incessant desire to render account to the Father; but as the Son of God, he has the simultaneous right and duty to administer, in his own authority, the Father's mandates and, as the Son of Man, to demonstrate to the Father the goodness of his creation by bringing about, on his behalf and in his sight, what is humanly good, correct, just, and loving.

The origin of the Son's mission lies in the mystery of eternity and cannot be comprehended. On the basis of its form, however, which is discernible to us in the Incarnation, we can say that Christ's mission and his desire to be sent (which coincide within his Divine Person) presuppose two things: the world as it has become through sin and heaven as it always was and always will be. Belonging to that heaven is the Father's will, which is subject to no variation at all during the entire period of Christ's life on earth. The criterion toward which the Son looks, and which constantly accompanies him as the Father's look, is one so eternal, universal, objective, and complete that the Son, who traverses his human path wholly within this will, can impart to that path all these heavenly qualities. No matter how finite and limited his human actions and sufferings may appear, they are in truth absolute; if we compare, for example, the Father's anger under the Old Covenant with the Son's anger under the New Covenant, then we understand that both spring from the same eternal source. Thus we can gauge, in faith, the profundity of the echo that the Lord's externally insignificant earthly existence sent through eternal heaven and how it was able to affect the relation between the Father and creation in its innermost essence.

VI

THE INCARNATE SON
BEFORE THE FATHER

The Son lives on earth initially as a child. Like every child, he learns to make his way in life, to adapt to the world around him, to accept and return the love of his fellow men. This early period, in the bosom of the family, is a quite protected one: his Mother and foster-father are holy persons; coldness, rejection, ill-feeling, and disappointment are spared the child. Nonetheless, even in this environment, the Son, who is God, comes to learn the difference between heaven and earth—which does not mean that he experiences human love (whose caring presence surrounds him) as something inferior or even just as something that is naturally his due, for he experiences this, in fact, as a love that aspires toward God, has as much purity as men can attain by the grace of God, and is thus already incipient Christian love. But as a God-man, who possesses the vision of the Father, he also has constant experience of the Father's love in its fullness and perfection, and he returns this not only to the Father but to the men around him, through an emanation that increases their love. By means of this increase, he sees at once what his filial love can do among men. While his Mother brings him up, and his foster-father teaches him the rudiments of life and work, he introduces them to love of himself and of the heavenly Father—in a wholly new way that they, the blessed, did not previously know. And the Father, from within heaven, sees this exchange and accompanies it with his blessing; he sees in his Son the fullness of being human, the culmination of his thoughts on creation. Mary and Joseph, too, are humans as he intended them to be: they are so because they live in the immediate sphere of his Son (who is God), loving him, allowing themselves to be enriched and guided by him, and gaining through him a share in the infinite love that exists in heaven.

At some time or other, as he grows up, he makes the acquaintance of evil, of that which rejects, and he gauges the distance that separates it from his Mother and Joseph. He can compare, in his heart, this No with the Yes of his Mother, but as a man, he must also look up to his Father and see what effect sin has upon him; he must endeavor to intercept this affront himself and bear the suffering it causes, must make the attempt, by interposing himself, to prevent it from reaching the Father's heart. Already now, when he is not yet proclaiming God's word and there can be no talk of converting men, he is waging his battle for God, in a way comparable to a small child's fighting for his father. Perhaps he understands that this new experience of man is only the concrete extension, and human appropriation, of an experience that he knows, as God, from eternity.

And he can, in this battle, already assess the effectiveness of his self-interposition: in his vision of the Father he can, as it were, read what his engagement for the Father achieves. He is far from wanting to assess this achievement as something in its own right; rather, he is only anxiously concerned to protect the Father and reveal him to the world in such a way that it sees him not merely as the strict, fear-inspiring judge but as the original source of all love.

And the Son prays. He prays to the Father; he learns from Mary and Joseph to say prayers but lends those prayers the divine depth that accords with his essence and office. And he experiences how the Father accepts and blesses his prayer—rising to him from within the world—rejoices in it, and sees his relationship to the world transformed by it. Christ's Church comes into being through this prayer. Despite the tranquillity that surrounds him, and his still not having experienced the wider world, his prayer is not merely that of one privileged individual, ascending directly and in isolation to God by virtue of its own special grace; rather, it is a prayer from the center of the world, from amidst the Father's creation, a prayer that gathers and includes not only the prayer of his parents but every halting prayer on earth and also attempts to embrace those who are still unaware of their obligation to pray.

Then there are the hard words, those that are directed at him personally, with the intention of wounding him. The experience of lovelessness, the insults, the hate. The hate is aimed at him but somehow always misses its mark, because the Father's presence protects him and because his mission is so great that it covers him like a shield and lends him the power to resist. He knows why he is there; he knows his task, and does not assess its value and scope in terms of everyday victories and defeats. It is safely lodged with the Father, and the Father assures its accomplishment. He has no need to concern himself about the nature of its unfolding; only to do what is demanded at every stage in the calm certitude of one who has been sent. He need only look to the Father in order to have this certitude instilled anew into his innermost life. And his external life derives such a fullness from this that it does not recoil from contradiction by other men but in fact integrates them, despite their resistance and without their comprehension, into his work.

And when the time arrives to leave his parents' home and become visible to all as the Father's sower, so much has already been invisibly sown, in the form of inner prayer, attitude, and will, that he can fall back on it in order to secure new sowing and provide a deeply fertile soil for its growth. Through the first disciples whom he gains and who become his followers, he experiences things that fill him with astonishment, because he rediscovers in them effects of heavenly radiance. It is the same astonishment that filled him as a child, when he observed Mary and Joseph at work or at prayer and in their general behavior. He discovers the new life in those souls, whose true possessor he is, whose secrets reveal themselves to him, always in living oneness with the watchful, accompanying Father in heaven, always with a view to him, in the confirmation that is given the Son by the Father. And his astonishment at the fact that men are able to hear and to follow his words is, in a way, boundless, because he is sufficiently a man to know men from the inside and because all the instances of self-overcoming, renunciation, and holiness he encounters fill him with respect for the power of the Father's grace.

In becoming a man, the Son receives, like every one of the Father's creatures, a body of the sort appropriate to him. He is not put into just any kind of matter whatsoever but assumes from the Virgin Mary the flesh that has been prepared for him. This body is for him the expression of an idea and a will of the Father's at the time of creation. He recognizes in it the Father's thoughts regarding his creature: what kinds of capacities and activities he had intended for it and also what limitations he had imposed. This body is something more to him than a companion: it belongs to him. Through living in it, he experiences what other men experience in their bodies; he comes to know the joys and sufferings of a bodily existence. As God, he knew about this from eternity; now he experiences it humanly. And in this human experience he remains a Divine Person. He makes use of his body in order to fulfill his mission: through it he converses with the apostles, preaches, and heals the sick; through it he can be weary or feel anger or shed tears or share in the enjoyment of a banquet. His tongue proclaims the word of the Father. He experiences the limitations inherent in a bodily existence, but he in no way senses this as being outside the truth or standing opposed to it; it belongs to the truths of the Father, forms a part of them.

In his fellow men, he sees how the body and the conditions of bodily life lead them astray into sin. And he wants to experience temptation in himself so as to know the way in which men are susceptible; he wants to chasten his body, to keep watch, to feel hunger. His flesh does not succumb to temptation but overcomes it: not just, however, because he is God in fleshly form, but because he is a man who obeys the Father fully. He is obedient right down to the smallest fibers of his body and thus actualizes, in that body, the full holiness of the Father.

When, on the evening before his Passion, he sits down at the table with his apostles in order to dispense to them the Eucharistic Meal of the New Covenant, he does so in the consciousness that, through this consummated sacredness, his Body and Blood are capable of becoming the legacy of his earthly life for all men: on earth for his Church and extending even into the sphere of eternal life. His life in the body was so wholly the revelation of the Father that it remains for all time an up-raised signpost, a sacrament that sustains a life in the faithful of such a kind that the Father is able to recognize in them the continued life of his Son. And he takes this element of recognition by the Father into account and builds on it.

But the eucharistic Son represents two sorts of things to the Father: the memory of the fallen Adam, in whose place he offered himself to the Father and whose flesh he inhabits, and the memory of the life of the Second Adam, who has taken on flesh in being born of the Virgin. Thus he is, at the same time, a sign of both the Father's justice and his love, but a justice whose final word is love. The Eucharist is a gift to Christians of unfathomable depth. It contains a mystery of eternal life but in eternal connection with the body and the Son's bodily experience. He has imparted to the sacrament the vision of the Father that he possessed when embodied. And because the Son knows, in that vision, that the Father accepts his sacrifice, he also has the certainty that the Father will everywhere recognize and accept him in his dispensed body. That the Father will not deny any man who steps before him with the password to heaven—the most powerful, because it is the flesh of the Son. This certainty is based not only on the Son's contribution through the Cross; it has its roots already in his human life prior to the Cross. The Passion will give him, in addition, the mystery of confession, by which the Eucharist is supplemented, for whoever consumes his Body and drinks his Blood must also be able to step forth in purity and show, by confession of his sins, that he understands in which respects he is impure.

Both sacraments contain the quintessence of all that the Son had experienced on earth. Confession contains all the sins that he met with and suffered for: that were the fault of others but that he had taken upon himself and expunged, through the absolution of the Cross, so definitively that the Father can recognize the Son's presence in the sacramental remission. The Eucharist also contains, once again, the quintessence of this life, but now as transferred to, and embodied in, men. And these two sacraments come together to form a new whole: inasmuch as there is now a concurrence between what the Son had experienced in his own bodily life and what he had experienced of sinners and, similarly, between the two experiences of the Son as the incarnate God and as the perfecter of the first Adam. Hence, in those who make confession and take Communion, the Father recognizes the confluence of his creation with the Incarnation of the Son, a confluence that he himself had planned at creation and that was realized by the Son on the Cross.

VII

THE FATHER AND THE CROSS

The hour of the Cross is the hour of the Father; for it is the hour that he alone knows. The Son, who could know it, forgoes that knowledge. One of the reasons the Father has reserved this knowledge for himself surely lies in the fact that the Son's obedience is to undergo the most severe testing possible. That is why he forgoes any form of obedience in which he would always know in advance what is to come and could prepare himself for that. Also, precisely the chosen sort of obedience allows the whole of the Son's freedom to assert itself at every moment of his life.

When he explicitly assures the apostles that no one, including the Son, knows the hour but the Father alone, he thereby shows the Father that he is taking no precautions to uncover the secret, that he is free to be utilized in whatever direction, free from preparing himself for any specific eventuality, free for everything the Father may command; that he does not give his word of obedience in a merely external way while internally surmising the Father's intentions and exerting control over them in his mind.

This most difficult of the Son's hours, which exists for him within this world and its transient time and thus itself bears the mark of transience, exists for the Father so much within the eternal that it is constantly before his eyes: he sees it coming; he holds it back for the time being. He will have to let it exert its full weight, will not be allowed to lighten it. During it, the divine Son must not receive so much support from the Father that he is unable to plumb the full depths of his human Passion. It must not be, for example, that the Son merely offers his body up for crucifixion, while his spirit remains so strongly attached to the Father that he endures his bodily torment by virtue of this anchoredness in the eternal. It must not be that he feels the nearness of the Father—indeed, flies so ardently toward him in spirit—that his suffering body becomes, so to speak, just a discarded husk, a miserable instrument, barely good enough to endure pain and be restored to life as a worthy human body only after the Resurrection.

The Father chooses the instruments of the Passion, and those instruments are sinful men. The Son will not suffer for abstract, theoretical sins: he will fall into the hands of real sinners. They are his enemies; they desire his death. They will scourge him, crown him with thorns, and nail him up. In all of this, they will have him in mind and will aim to affect him. He will be the object of men's attack. In their sin, they have chosen this man as their target, but only because they are rebelling, via him, against God. Against the God of creation and against the God of Christian teaching and faith. Therefore every dimension of the Son's being—

the physical as well as the spiritual, the commonly human as well as the specially God-human—is subjected to suffering in the same way, is struck with the same unerring accuracy. Since the Son, as a sinless man, embodies the spirit of unfallen mankind and, in his human nature, represents the Father on earth, and since he has accepted that representative role out of love and wants to suffer for God out of love and also places his entire divine being at disposal out of love, his whole concern therefore tends toward wanting to feel every blow of suffering in its full intensity. He asks for nothing but lets nothing be lost of whatever is offered.

He must recognize in this hour the hour of the Father, just as the Father must recognize in it his Son. This will happen through the Father's withdrawing his presence from him, while the Son, who is about to enter the ultimate darkness, sends back his spirit to him by committing it into his hands—hands that are, in his sense of total abandonment, no longer perceptible to him. The Father accepts this spirit but gives no sign to show that he has received it. However, the Father loves the Son so much that he carefully retains everything the Son deposits with him, in order to return it again at his glorification. He is the administrator of the Son's goods, just as he was the administrator of his mission, and as, at the same time, he is also the administrator of his own unbending divine will, which would be modified if he were to permit any lessening of the suffering. To the extent that the Son suffers completely, the

Father must remain completely true to his eternal re-
solve, completely true to the Son's mission, and completely participative in it, precisely when his nearness
has become invisible to the Son. The veiling of the
Father imparts the final note of the absolute to his
divine isolation.

It is hardly comprehensible to us how the Son could
long to realize so radical an obedience and how the Father could have conceded him this. But we can imagine
a father entrusting his child with some major task to
be performed independently and then restraining himself—at the point where difficulties begin to mount—
from any intervention, such as coming forward with
suggestions or even taking things in hand himself (just
to show the child that he is standing by and keeping
an eye on everything). Thus the divine Father, too,
does not want to intervene in the Son's work, whose
ultimate independent task is his extreme obedience on
the Cross. This obedience, which he has freely under-
taken, is something he must suffer through in freedom
if the independence of his mission is to be preserved
and, indeed, if the elements of independence and obedience in his mission are to coincide. His achievement
is not merely to suffer the Cross but to endure the
suffering of the Cross in the form of obedience the
Father has determined. And this obedience is shaped
most utterly when the shaping hand is invisible. When
everything—every moment, every advancing second
—remains veiled, left entirely to the Father's will. In

none of the Son's words does he ask: Why hast thou permitted this? But only: Why hast thou forsaken me? The Father draws back so purely that what is purest in the Son is able to come forward in his suffering. And he really is the Father; he shows here what the most fatherly of all tasks can be, what a father's responsibility toward his son can be burdened with.

We observe this drama, up to the very end, with human eyes, in a faith that remains linked to human standards. We have no other choice. At the same time, we learn that our greatest possible efforts to understand prove inadequate to this mystery but also that this failure is no reason to abandon our efforts. Everything is infinitely greater than our comprehension, because it is, after all, divine, and because the aspects that are accessible to us are only aspects. God seems to leave them with certain definite contours, so that our conceptual thought does not lose its edge, but at the same time he shows that they are only aspects of something infinite, so that none of our concepts remains tied to the human level.

∼

The Son's divine-human suffering presents to the Father a human side that leads to temporal death and a divine side (as the Son is, of course, God) that imparts a boundlessness to his suffering. In both, the Son reveals himself to the Father: as the man who assumed respon-

sibility for the succession of Adam and as the God who
accepted the redemptive task from the Father. Both of
these radiate, in inseparable combination, back toward
the Father and in so doing evidence his origin from
the Father. The Father recognizes the Son whom he
generates from eternity, and he also recognizes in him
the man whom he has created. Implicit in this recognition is the whole history of mankind, which turns away
from the Father and whose sins are borne summarily
by the Son; and also the whole life of the Son, who is
turned toward him and went to the Cross out of love
for the Father's world. Thus we find here a twofold
oppositional unity: first the bringing together of the
acts of eternal generation by the Father and temporal
creation by the Father; then the bringing together of
the two polar extremes of creation, namely, the sum of
all evil and the outweighing counter sum of all good;
and this unified totality is placed in the Father's hands
by the Son's infinite love.

The knowledge of the Cross is just as much a knowledge of the absolute fatherhood of the Father as of the
absolute sonship of the Son: both are copresent so that,
in the abandoned Son, the Father must recognize—
indeed, wishes to recognize—himself as the one who
approved the Son's mission and is the recipient of his
love. That this love must undergo such suffering is explained by the fact that mankind had fallen from grace
and deserved God's judgment; and more profoundly
still, that the Son, through his representative bearing

of this fallenness and judgment, has won grace back —restored and even heightened, gratuitously as pure grace—for mankind. The Son has taken away the sins of mankind in order to give, precisely from mankind's position of remoteness from the Father, the supreme proof of his love for the Father. Thus everything comes together—what was, what is, and what will be—in the presence of the Son who hangs from the Cross. He is the whole history of mankind, but also the whole history of God's grace along with it. Suffering and death are therefore an end only from the earthly point of view —to God, they are a midpoint, which extends right through the center of the Father; for the Son does not cease, even in dying, to be generated by him and to convey his eternal gratitude to him, in a love that expresses its utmost intensity precisely now. The Son's death is the exemplification of the supreme aliveness of triune love; it does not alter the relationship between the Father and the Son; the Father does not need to interrupt the eternal act of generation in order to enable the Son's death. One can say only that the Son's sonship reaches its supreme temporal exemplification in his redemptive death. In the life of a human father, there comes the moment when he discovers that his son has grown up: is equal in stature to him, a free, mature personality, no longer requiring to be supervised and guarded. And if it is true that the eternal Son accomplishes the Father's will even on the Cross, it is also true—humanly speaking—that the eternal Father has never had to leave the Son so much to his own will as here.

In the Cross, we can discern no one clear meaning in terms of earthly life; here, it is as if all the stages of the Son's life—childhood, youth, adulthood—become somehow intermixed, not in confusion, but as the result of a supreme divine order, which is also capable of imparting a new order to the world. The fruitfulness of the Father, who generates the Son in an eternal act of procreation, undergoes no diminishment during the Passion but rather its consummate glorification: since not only does the fruit itself (the Son) demonstrate its own fruitfulness by redeeming the world, but that reflects, in turn, on the fruitfulness of the Father, inasmuch as creation, too, now blossoms into a new fruitfulness.

But God had imposed a sentence of burdensome work on man: man is to live by the toil of his hands, and woman is to give birth in pain; that is what justice demands in response to sin. This punishment takes on its highest form in the burdensome work of the Cross. The Son invented no new law for himself in relation to sin; he did not distance himself from the Father's words to Adam and Eve but subjected himself to the very same law. He himself submits to this decreed form of punishment and imparts an ultimate meaning to it, an ultimate gravity, and an ultimate response. Adam and Eve had heard the words and had allowed the punishment to be imposed on them without being able to take any preventive steps. The Son, however, heard the words in a new way, in love; and that new hearing immediately supplied the response of love. The Cross is the sign that, in his hearing, he had also well understood something that had remained largely unintelligible to the first man. He understood this for the first time, not at the moment of the Passion, but already when the words were directed to the first humans, when the Father allowed his voice to be heard, which reverberated through the world but was fully apprehended only in heaven. Something that had existed already then in heaven now experiences, in this earthly death, its ultimate fulfillment, and the Father recognizes in that death the consummation of the content of his words. He recognizes this just as he recognizes in that death the consummation of the world's fall into sin. What has taken place in heaven and on earth since the expulsion from paradise merges into oneness in the dying body of the Lord.

~

Also inherent in the Cross, however, is a revelation of heaven itself, namely, a countenance that the triune God in heaven has acquired in view of the world's fall into sin. The Son, who now suffers in his human nature, made the decision for this as God; the God in him had lowered himself in order to become man and to suffer. The total humiliation of the Son of Man on the Cross includes not just the reality of guilty and suffering humanity but certainly, too, the concrete reality of the insults that had been perpetrated against God in his heaven. A mere man could not possibly bear the responsibility for the world's guilt before the Father, even if he were to give up his life in the attempt: What would this human life be in relation to the straying of all, the forlornness of all? For that reason alone, the Son must be God on the Cross.

But the divine element inherent in the Son is not, of course, merely his own: it belongs inseparably to the Father and the Spirit as well. Hence, in the ignominy done to the Son, the Father directly recognizes the ignominy that was inflicted on him as the Father and all the insults that were aimed at the Holy Spirit. And it is, in fact, implicit in the meaning of this sin that the sinners, through their murderous act against the Son, also wish to strike at the Father; and that the Son carries, in his dying, an intended shielding of God from this. The Father recognizes this aim of the sinners in every specific aspect of the Passion, not merely in a summary way, but with full concreteness of detail. But because the Father's view of the coming Resurrection, like that of the Incarnation or of the Son's eternal existence in heaven, is never obscured for a moment, he sees through the Cross to its consequences with eternal finality. He sees the sin but also its expiation. And the expiation that is offered him by the Son outweighs the sin, because the whole force of divine love is directly opposed to evil, infinite love to ultimately finite evil: indeed, because ultimately the whole of eternal heaven stands confronted by the aberrant world. This confrontation had already begun at the first hour and had been carried on for thousands of years until it reached its decisive climax here. The death of the Son on the Cross is the unambiguous victory of God's love over the sins of the world.

The event of the Passion cannot be exhaustively reduced to conceptual terms. One could compare it, metaphorically, with a painful operation whose purpose was the eradication of a fatal illness. That view would not be false; but the mysterious aspect of the Son's devotion to the Father, of overflowing triune love—the very essence of the matter—would remain unexpressed. And although one could think up many similar images, all would fail to capture the decisive element. For it involves something unique, indescribable: the fact that the image God the Father intended to create of himself in man ultimately acquires the dimensions of the image of the Son and is therefore more than any human image. It is a question of the super-image in the non-image.

～

"He who has seen me has seen the Father." The Son possesses a kind of transparency through which the Father can be seen. And it belongs to the most essential part of his mission to represent the Father. But one cannot say, in the proper sense, that he is the Father's "image", for he is identical in essence with the Father yet distinct in his Person from him. One living creature can engender another that has the same essence as its own, but it cannot bring forth an "image" of itself. The Son is the second Person of the triune God, and even in the revealing of the Father through the Son, the Father remains the first Person. One who looks at the incarnate Son does not see a replica of the Father, just as one who looks at the Father through the Son does not see in him a likeness of the Son. Their identity of essence prohibits them from standing opposed to each other in the relation of object and replica. Hence, vision of the Father is not limited to vision of the Son, and the mystery of the Cross is therefore made possible, in which the Father was never so clearly recognizable although also never so inaccessibly concealed.

Whoever sees the Son on the Cross sees the Father. But the presence of the Father on the Cross, as visible through the suffering Son, is not open to our line of sight: the Cross stands between and blocks it. In a sense, the Son now possesses a transparency that discloses the Cross upon which he is nailed, while the Father is concealed by the Cross. But there is no possibility of getting past the Cross, of going beyond the image of the Cross, and looking at the Father so as to experience more of him. And yet the Father is present on the Cross; he is, of course, the one who has aban-

doned the Son and made him abandoned. But this abandonment is like a veil in which the Father wraps himself. From all eternity, the triune God had envisaged
that the Son on the Cross should feel, not the soothing
hand of the Father, but only the hard wood. And thus
we see, through the Son, a Father whom, in the end,
we do not see; who evidences his presence through absence; who, in order to leave the Son to his own will,
has completely veiled himself and allows the Son's call
to echo into emptiness. This emptiness is no longer like
that of the desert into which the Son had gone, which
was an embodiment of the emptiness of the earth and of
being alone in the world. Such loneliness left room for
nothing but God. The Son on the Cross is no hermit;
he is now the chosen one, with whose will the Father
is so compliant that there can no longer be any talk of
a willing and deciding by the Son, because these are
fulfilled beyond all measure. In this sense, the Father
becomes visible on the Cross, in the framework of
the consummate suffering of Golgotha; but the fullness
comes through the abandonment, the seeing through
the lack of visibility. There is no concept, no product
of fancy, not even an instilled belief that could convey
an authentic "image" of the Father here.

God once created man in his own image and likeness, and we can look for traces of that image in every man by trying to sense in his nature and life something of the Father's intention, some reflection of the
divine. In the crucified Son, however, the divine has

disappeared so much behind the human, is so with-
drawn from any gaze, that the time of the image is
gone. The time when God's eye rested on Cain is also
past here. Only this one thing remains valid: the complete will of the Father in the complete surrender of
the Son; and, implicit in that, the demand on us to be
coinvolved in that surrender. For the Father now leaves
the Son to his filial will, and as a result of that leaving,
that letting go of, the Son transfers the image-world
of creation above and beyond itself into a nonimage.
And yet the fatherhood of the Father was never more
distinct, never more earnest, than at this hour of the
Cross. What he bequeathed to the Son—his mission
with its path through the world—has now become
fully the Son's possession, something the Son has accomplished so utterly that the Father's will has been
fully realized and made apparent in the Son; while the
Father himself withdraws into absence, so as to enable
all the light to fall upon the Son, indeed, so as to take
undistracted cognizance of what the Son is. The divine
unity of essence is not for one moment shattered; the
Son's equal standing with the Father is fully evidenced
and not for one moment called into question; while
the distinctness of the Persons has never been more
clearly revealed than in the relationship between the
Son who is abandoned and the Father who abandons
him.

VIII

THE FATHER AND
THE RESURRECTION

The Son, who describes himself as the way, the truth, and the life, also says that he does nothing of himself but only what the Father shows him. His life is a life stemming from the Father, for even in eternity all life has its everlasting origin in the Father. And the Father gave the Son a human life, a life quite similar to the one he gave Adam. The life of the Son can be regarded as a resumption of the life of Adam, which did not seem to the Son too paltry a thing to be lived.

But Adam had to die and was able to do nothing to counter death. The Son, by contrast, brings life from the Father, and the resurrections that he effected during his lifetime are signs of this. Of course those resurrected arise to the same transient form of life they had lived before; but all this serves to make evident, in principle, the Son's power over death. Now, when the Son himself has died, the Father resurrects him. He does not resurrect him in order to restore him to divine life, since the divine relationships among the Persons are not affected by the Son's death. He resurrects him for the purpose of making him the firstborn among the dead and of demonstrating anew, through a miracle that bursts the confines of human reason, that he himself is the source of the bestowal of all life. For the Father bestows this life on the Son, not according to the laws laid down by him for creation, but in a way contrary to them all, inasmuch as he makes life out of death: out of the death of the Crucified, as something confirmable by us, the life of the Resurrected, as also confirmable by us. And he positions us, as witnesses, at the center of this miracle, as witnesses together with the Holy Spirit—immediately involved witnesses, taken by surprise in their understanding, who must acknowledge the incomprehensible leap, the breaking through death, without being able to explain it. But in the life of God nothing has been broken through. We have seen the Son's corpse lying in the tomb, and now we see (through the eyes of the disciples) the Resurrected; we know that, between his previous and present lives lies the dead one's descent into hell, and we almost feel that we should overlook, should forget, that fact, so that the two ends of his life will fit evenly together. And the gap is closed yet not closed—so little can we nullify the distance between God's essence and our faith, between the Holy Spirit's knowledge and our knowledge in the Spirit.

The hour that the Father chose for the creation of man is known to him alone; suddenly something was there that was not previously there. The hour that the Father chooses for the awakening of the Son is undoubtedly also the Father's hour, but it is simultaneously related—since it comes after the Son's hour—to the succession of hours within human history. There is a relationship of conditionality here: in order that the Father's hour could come, the Son's hour had to precede it; in order to reach the point of Resurrection, he had to have died on the Cross. Indeed, in order to receive his new life from the Father, he had to have lived the life of the first Adam, to have entered into human history. The Son calls himself "the resurrection and the life"; by linking these two words with an "and", he indicates that they do not refer simply to identical things. Only in him are the two one. The Father brings this unity about by restoring life to the Son through the Resurrection, through which the Son, in turn, can become the resurrection for his fellow men. And the life that he receives is not divine but human life. He had, of course, died as a man; the Father had taken this human life back to himself, and now he breathes it forth again, infused with the everlastingness of its origin.

When a sinner died as a result of his sin and his part in the world's guilt, he had to place himself in the arms of the Father without any sort of surety for his hope to be resurrected to eternal life. What God would do with him remained unknown to him. But now the one who has died is he who had freely entered into his death out of love for sinners; and regarding that death the sinner knows that the Father has taken it up and transformed it into everlasting life. The Son's Resurrection attests to this. But if all things have been created with a view to the Son, then not only is Christian life now lived with a view to the Son, but death, too, may be died with a view to him, as oriented through his death toward his Resurrection. And with this our hope for eternal life has obtained, in faith, a definite form and palpability. Through the Resurrection, we are to experience just how powerful and boundless the Father's life is. And through the return of the Resurrected to us, through his forty days on earth, not only are the sacraments to be consummated—which now become infused with both divine and divine-human life—but also our belief in eternal life is to become a genuine, irrefutable human experience. The disciples see, hear, and touch the Lord; they see him, not up in heaven seated at the right hand of the Father, but just as concretely present among themselves as they saw him concretely die on the Cross. Thus he becomes for them the resurrection.

∼

A person who converts to faith undergoes the experience of having his life given a new meaning; not just because everything has become richer and he is permitted to live with an abiding sense of hope that is always being newly fulfilled in Christian terms, but precisely because this new meaning of life is a meaning in God, a conferral of meaning through God. It is realized in a process of exchange that God mediates, but one the believer never wholly comprehends and of which, in fact, he becomes conscious only when he is not seeking to understand it exactly and to determine his own exact position vis-à-vis God. He finds himself in a state of suspension before God; he lives a human life and yet does not live it, he can say with Paul: "It is no longer I who live, but Christ who lives in me."

This existence in suspension is simultaneously a state of prayer. Through his personal prayer—and perhaps just as much through the wealth of the Church's prayer, through his experiencing the radiance of the prayers of others—man remains in a state of openness toward God; he allows the Spirit to blow; he keeps his soul so it can be pervaded; his actions come under the in fluence of this sort of contemplative posture. But his reception of meaning from God, his allowing himself to be given authentic life by God, has its centerpoint in the Resurrection of the Son.

This can be inferred already from the resurrection of Lazarus. He has died; and his sisters appeal to the Lord, about whom they know, in faith, that he possesses the power. The Lord reveals that power; and the new life that he confers stems from him, is his own. In a special way, Lazarus could have applied Paul's words to his own case. He comes to life by virtue of the force of the Lord's call, of his voice, of his being the Word. He arises because he has heard and responded to that call, and this response itself was effected by the power of the call. Those witnesses who are present understand that the higher one, the Lord, imparts life to the deceased out of his own aliveness. And now something similar happens to the Son himself, and this time the higher one who enables the deceased to arise is the Father. It is a mystery so exalted that no man was present at the moment of Resurrection. The witnesses to his arising can experience this event only as the highest mystery of their faith, as an over-fulfillment of all the petitions of the Mother and the apostles, and as a testimony to an unending transcendent life of the Father, from whom the risen Son also receives all life.

The world of obedience, the world of prayer, the world of action and contemplation all point back to the Father. The Father has taken the Son's life back to himself in order to dispense it in a new way from his divine source, to allow it to pass through his heavenly aliveness and shine forth anew in the world with all the qualities of heavenly life. Thus the Son's eternal generation by the Father has entered a new phase for men: that of taking on a certain visibility to the world, even if the core of the mystery is not laid bare. Within the Son's gloriously self-revealing humanity, the element of divine life has ultimately gained predominance: it has become an instrument for the revelation of triune love. Thus the Resurrection of the Son takes place, not primarily for his sake or for the sake of his mission, but out of love for men, for whom his whole mission was intended. It was for the sake of their new life in God that the Father had allowed the Son to sacrifice himself on the Cross and for the sake of this life that he brought about his Resurrection.

When men speak of love, when they have the experience of loving another or many others, they believe they are speaking of something that is part of their own mental experience, something they are themselves capable of ordering and controlling. In view of the Son's Resurrection, however, it must become clear to them just how much everything that belongs to them, including their love, is only fragmentary. The man who comes from God brings them their own fulfillment. God is truth, and they themselves are, at best, emblems of that truth; God is love, and what they call love is, at most, a pale reflection of that love. They are the symbols for whom God the Father has effected the great symbol of the Resurrection. With this pivotal event, their lives first acquire real meaning, now that God the Father has revealed something of the meaning of his eternal essence in the Son's magnificence, has allowed something of the meaning of his life to shine through the Son's life and become visible in it—and this life is now truly love. Everything now lets itself be dissolved into love, and the symbols of love, along with those of life, are so distinct that they do not blur into some vague general conception and can still, while no longer having any limitations, present as many countenances as God wishes to lend them. And there is a great va-

riety of those, so that men of every kind might grasp
something of this.

~

When, in the beginning, the Creator brought forth
living man, his breath was infused into his creature.
That which constitutes man's life bears the mark of
his origins in God. But it is not itself divine life. God
the Creator establishes a particular relationship between
himself and his creature, the nature of which he leaves,
in part, to be determined by the latter: he is allowed to
speak with him and, through conversation with him, to
keep the relationship alive and to renew it—a relationship of faith oriented toward constantly new obedience
and new knowledge and love. God and creature both
have their lives, and the creaturely life unfolds within
a relationship established by God and maintained by
man.

With the Resurrection of the Son, the Father once
again confers new life; however, it is no longer a life
externally positioned before God, but a life in the mystery of deepest union. The Father confers this life upon
that Son who had already possessed a divine and a human life, that Son who, during his human life, had already brought his friend Lazarus back from the dead.
All who were present understand this as a work of love;
in fact, however, it was a work of love effected, not by
the Lord alone, but also by the sisters who helped to

condition this resurrection through their prayer and suffering. The Son is characterized as the one who can raise the dead and will rise from the dead on the third day. There is often talk of this special attribute, even at the time when the Lord appears before his judges. He himself characterizes himself as the resurrection and the life. To those who receive his word and partake of his Body, he promises resurrection on the Judgment Day. He alludes to this quality of his, which now comes to the fore in what he says about himself and whose full implications will later become visible in the Church and at the end of time. It is with this quality that he enters into death and submits himself to the Father for Resurrection. He is the one who already possesses what the Father will present to him. He bears this quality as a "sign pointing toward the Father", comparable to the sign that is inherent in creatures insofar as they have been created with a view to the Son, to that mystery of directionality that is given them as they embark on their paths and remains an expectation until the day when it is transformed into complete realization. One cannot, of course, claim that the Father had been waiting for this sign in the Son. Still, he reserved the hour (which was his hour) to himself, as a strictly kept secret hidden from even the Son, in order to reveal it to him when the hour had come—not in miracles or shows of favor, but in the severity and abandonment of the Cross. And the Son accepts the Cross and suffers it through, while the sign of the Resurrection that attaches to him remains alive in him even in death and, indeed, takes on a new life precisely through his suffering. The Father then accepts this and takes up the truth of the Son's self-characterization in order to turn that truth into the life of the Resurrection. The circle is thus closed, but not apart from the Son's dependence on the Father and on the hour that is known to the Father alone.

Yet the sign is also just as essentially a "sign pointing toward men", and the Father has revealed the sign—known to and preserved by him and now become the fulfilled Resurrection—to men in order to renew their faith and give it the quality of a faith in the living, risen Son. During his days on earth, the Son stood in a particular relation to men. In a posture of dialogue, a conversation that had been initiated and would never be broken off. The men who listened to him were able, through his words and his miracles, to deepen their belief. Nonetheless, everything took place within a certain atmosphere of mutual freedom: the men could express their agreement or distance themselves; they were like spectators at some event. This situation is changed once the Son bears the sins of all on the Cross, has instituted the Eucharist and confession, and rises from the dead. His position toward men is now different: they no longer stand side by side with him, but he carries them within himself. And therefore they must, in faith, implicitly recognize in his Resurrection the sign of their own resurrection. He has risen before them so that they might rise before him and recognize in him that which he has conferred on them, in order to refine, transform, and offer it as something pure to the Father. The Father, who accepts what is offered, receives the risen Son as one of us and, at the same time, takes him away from us. This dual movement is now realized in the Son. But both movements are directed toward the Father and carry us within them. The Resurrection is like an espousal with the human race, in relation to which the Incarnation can be seen as the engagement. Something has been transmuted, in its innermost essence, into a complete unity. Just as the sign of the husband is impressed on the wife in a consummated marriage, as a complete secret between the spouses that is completely self-evident for them, so the Resurrection is the mysterious secret between the Son and his Bride before the Father, who sees and knows.

IX

THE FATHER AND THE CHURCH

The Christian mysteries on earth, which all go back
to the triune mysteries in God, must be accessible to
men. In each one, men should discern something that
was revealed for their sake. They should feel themselves attracted, but even more: they should gain objective knowledge that God is willing to bestow things
constantly upon them and to draw them toward himself
in a manner adapted to their human powers of comprehension.

Thus the mystery of the Virgin Birth is one directed
fully toward God; yet it contains many aspects that are
fully meant for men and that they can use as a basis
for gaining insight into things that would otherwise
never have become intelligible to them. It is a mystery
of the Son of Man with his Mother and at the same
time one of the preredemption of the Mother with
a view to the redemption of the world. The protec-
tion of Mary from original sin is, for all of us, an invitation to purity, the grace of redemption, and the
mystery of the Cross. Within the order of God's Incarnation, virginity and the Cross are bases for a variety of
profound relations, which become constantly evident
in the Son's life and also illumine the succession of

apostles and all the faithful. They do not shift restlessly back and forth between Birth and Cross but point to a unity that is implicit in the whole of the Son's life, forming both its beginning and its end. The virginal birth is no empty renunciation by the Mother, and also no senselessly imposed sacrifice; it is an anticipatory opening into the ever-greater fruitfulness of the Cross; and when the Son effects this opening, and alludes to it, and both invites and introduces his own to entry into it, then he also draws into it all his own mysteries —his existence as such and his miracles, his preaching and his conversations, his prayer—and he builds out of this an integrated structure that is intended for everyone: the Church. This means that his Mother becomes a Bride. In order to be able to become this, she has to share in the hour of the Cross but always remains able to return to the mystery of the virginal birth that was bestowed on her and is her own. And this is not a return to mere reflection or memory, but a return to the constantly renewed assurance of God's present gift, which is never lost to her: the fruitfulness to which she gave her assent for once and forever and the fact of her being included most obediently in the Son's love, in a life that transcends her but to which she gives her consent: a life that was instilled in her by the triune God, that she does not attempt to resist, and for which she holds ready all her reserves of strength. The suffering of the Son, her accompaniment of him, the excessive demands placed on her—all these things allow her to become the Son's Bride, while, at the same time, they allow the mystery of the Church to ripen in her and to arise out of her. Her most secret mysteries become the public mysteries of the Church, her concealed thoughts the laws of the faith, her relationship to her Son a standard to which every believer is subject. But the more the Son utilizes her to build his Church, and the more he bestows himself lavishly on this Church, the greater the gift to the Father becomes.

The Son has become so much a man that he constructs his Church in association with his Mother and his saints—in whom there can also be something of the nonsaintly. In this Church, the Father can now discern the purpose and benefit of the Incarnation and also recognize the structure from the Old Covenant, although revitalized through the love that the Son has received. He finds his own fatherly love reflected in her, and all the gifts of the Holy Spirit, and all the signs of the Son's love for him and the world; and he finds in all her members—from the Mother through to the last of sinners—all the signs of their affiliation with him, having passed through the Son. And for him, all the sacraments are bound up with the life of the Son, filled with his earthly days yet also radiant with his eternal days, inasmuch as they contain what the Father intends to bestow on men in eternity and, similarly, what the Father bestows on the Son from eternity. All the Church's shortcomings, her inadequacies, faults, and blemishes, are, however, dissolved in the immaculate being of the virginal Bride; and all the guilt of sinners is exorcised in confession in such a way that the penitents find their place beneath the Son's Cross. And the children who are baptized and receive at that moment something of the purity of the Child Jesus, and the dying who are given extreme unction and made ready for eternal life, and the married couples who have resolved to lead a life in the Church, and the priests who allow themselves to be ordained, and all those who have once been confirmed will no doubt all find, at one time or another, that shortcomings like their own also exist in the Church. But the Father will behold her through the all-purifying medium of the Son's Cross and discern in every received sacrament the radiant obedience of the Son. For him, the Church will become a perpetual interpretation of what the Son has accomplished, an image that has, for him, substance and lastingness and magnificence, because the Son's time overcomes our time, his human nature outshines ours, his love interposes itself before any weakening in our love in order to strengthen it through assimilation to his own power.

∼

Whenever the triune God exerts some effect on the world from within his heaven, each of the Persons sees his own part as linked to those of the others in a complete unity, which corresponds to the essential unity of their triune love. It is not necessary to make continual distinctions among the wishes, intentions, and achievements of the Father, the Son, and the Spirit, because they are always one, always concordant, arising out of one another and returning into one another. During the Son's sojourn on earth, he is, for the world, God made visible and sent by the Father, who enjoys, even as a man, the vision of the Father; whereas, for the Father, he is the Son in human form, who works and suffers in the vineyard of his creation, who, while able to see him, still seeks him in his life as a man and who wishes to be fully a man even in his relationship to the Father. He allows himself to be tempted, feels fear and revulsion on the Mount of Olives and abandonment on the Cross. Thus the exposition of the Son is a twofold one: in relation to men and in relation to the Father. For the Father and the Spirit, his activity takes on the special stamp of one who is bound to human form yet, at the same time, as the Son of God, constantly translates that form into the divine. And the scope of this activity is so wide as to encompass both his performance of miracles, through which he reveals the divine authority, and his suffering, through which he illustrates the complete devotion of the obedient man and becomes an exemplary model of faith. And there are also the festivities that he celebrates among men, the supper at which the beloved disciple leans on his breast; genuine earthly joys, but celebrated in a Christian way, joys that the Father bestows and that are anticipatory of heavenly bliss.

The sufferings and joys, the works and preachings of the Son are unique but formed in such a way that the Church can take them over in order to weave together her ecclesiastical year, to introduce the dates of the eternal into transient time, and to celebrate the Son's perpetual return to her midst in his birth, Passion, and Resurrection. She takes possession of the Gospels that have been entrusted to her and administers them in such a way that today's faithful can come to share in the events that were linked to him, in his activity and his truth. And when the Father observes the Church, he sees in her a summarized life history of the Son; he sees something that—in itself perhaps incomplete and lacking in power, but invigorated and reinforced through the breath of the Holy Spirit—continues the work of the Incarnation; he also sees the striving of the faithful to draw ever nearer to the mysteries of the Son, to encounter in them the Father, and to welcome in them the living Spirit. The tightly structured ecclesiastical year, with its internal variations as occasioned by the celebration of particular saints and the concrete administration of the sacraments, constitute together— in their form and interplay, their elements of juxtaposition and mutual fructification—a supremely vital life: the life of Christianity within the structured Church. As much as that life may draw sustenance from the life of the Son, it nevertheless also contains the life of imperfect men, of those who are striving and are always being replaced by newer generations. And God recognizes in this the whole of his creature: its turning away and the attempts of its love. The Church does not, after all, function in the manner of a sieve, which would sift the good from the bad, would effect a strict selection; but more like a melting pot, in which everything is thrown together and makes a united effort to live from God's grace. The Church is vested with grace. She lives from the grace of the living Lord but no less from the grace of the Father, who gives her his sanction, and the grace of the Spirit, who blows through her. She is the locus of an encounter with eternity, indeed, quite actually the locus of the beginning of life, the beginning of eternity in the midst of time. Man is drawn into this origin, shaken to the core in it and converted, enriched, and at the same time made poorer. Within it, he gauges constantly anew what the Lord is, what distance separates him from sinners; he comes to feel his own powerlessness, sees also the consummate powerlessness of the Lord, which is the source of all grace, and understands that there can be no comparison between the two. And yet he knows that his existence in the Church is nothing but grace and love and that even the feeling of his powerlessness is an instance of the Lord's grace, a gift in view of his poverty, and a sign by which the Father recognizes him. All seeking of God, all consciousness of being found by God, being loved and attempting to love in return, receiving life and passing it on to others—all this is the ecclesiastical process. A process upon which the Father must look if it is to be able to take place. The more Christian, the more Christlike, the Church is, the more dependent she must be upon the Father, since the Son keeps nothing for himself but brings everything to the Father, including, most of all, his Church.

~

Through the Cross, the Father gauges the extent of the Son's love, given that the Son calls out for him when he no longer possesses him, that the Son has not forgotten his name when he has nonetheless been abandoned by the Father. When, then, as a consequence of this suffering, the Son institutes the sacrament of confession, the Father sees how broad a door has thus been built into the Church: the door through which sinners enter in order to be cleansed and integrated into the communion of saints. But the Father, too, with the love of the Son and the Spirit together, cleanses those who arrive in his heaven after death and are to be given participation in his eternal life and his purity. And this eternal life is not something locked up within itself but is open toward the world and strives with all its powers for increased purity within the Church. Between the inhabitants of heaven and the Church there exist lasting ties, insofar as heaven draws the Church toward itself and dwells in a state of never-ending contemplation of what the Son has done and instituted.

When a man comprehends for the first time what the Church mediates to him, when he beholds the fullness of the sacraments and is allowed to share in the Church's wealth of prayer and move within the sphere of the one prayer that is there for him, then he feels the Church's unsuspected breadth and sees that neither her laws nor her deficiencies constitute a boundary for her or hold her back, but that her dimensions extend upward into heaven. This breadth is the result of the Cross. Prior to the institution of confession, any man who encountered the Lord had to acknowledge his guilt to him, or at least allow himself to be told about what was not as it should be with him, and thus he was cleansed. In the process, he might well have gained the impression that there was a certain accidental quality about his encounter with the Lord: that he, as this particular individual, just happened to be standing there when the Lord passed, but it could just as easily have been someone else standing there instead. Through the Cross and confession, however, this appearance of particularization and randomness has faded: everyone may now encounter the Lord; everyone may confess to him in order to be relieved of sins; everyone can, in the communion of the Church, find the narrow gate. The Father alone knows what price the Son has paid for the erection of that gate; he alone, too, knows what importance it possesses as the ever-new passageway to the Church. It is undoubtedly baptism that incorporates one into the Church and eradicates original sin; but man's perpetual inclination to sin required, over and above that, the institution of confession, and its acknowledging disclosure of sin seemed so important to God that he transferred it even into his eternity. One could, from the standpoint of the Cross, regard the institution of Purgatory as a transference of the confessional situation from the this-worldly context of the earthly Church to that of judgment in the next world;[1] one could see this as a case in which an institution of redemption and of the Church has affected, and been expanded into, the order of the Father; and nothing can bring more bliss to the Son than seeing his work glorified by the Father in this way.

When a man reflects on his life—how fleeting his days are, how futile his labors—and nevertheless attempts to keep alive, at length and steadily, his thoughts of God and his prayers, he has the consolation of knowing that he is attempting to realize, within the earthly sphere of the Church, something that succeeds eternally in the heavenly one and that his transient time thereby has a place in the eternal time of the Father. From the moment of creation to the end of the world, the Father is occupied with making heaven ready for men, with continuing his creative act in the direction of redemption and glorification. This allows men to recognize that they should not interpret their creaturely life, in its

[1] On this, cf. the author's still unpublished book on Purgatory. —ED.

transitional movement toward heaven, as anything but a symbol of what awaits them once they are with the Father. When they then arrive at their goal, they will find there not only the never-to-be-lost contemplation of triune love but also the perfected Church, which had been growing toward that goal while on earth, and that look of the Father's that has always rested, and will eternally rest, on her. The unity between transient and eternal time is assured through this sort of beholding of the Church. A vista is opened into the perfect, and on the basis of what he beholds, the looker finally grasps the perfection of the earthly Church, whose countenance had appeared to him deeply overshadowed by his own and others' sins. His piecemeal seeing and grasping becomes, in heaven, a perfected seeing and grasping, which exerts a retroactive effect on the earthly Church, and whose scope is so widened, through the vision of the triune God and of the sustaining of the Son's entire redemptive work by the Father, that much of what seemed incomprehensible on earth now reveals itself, in divine truth, as the supreme fullness.

X

THE FATHER AND
THE SACRAMENT

Before the Church acquires her visible form, she already has an existence in the Son; what occurs around him and in him is the material out of which she is to develop. He who is God on earth is also the developing Church on earth. After the Cross, however, he is within the Church on earth. A reversal has taken place: the Church is no longer in the Lord; the Lord is in her. The connections between them have not thereby become less close. These connections can now be defined in terms of the sacraments. They signify a constantly new breaking through of heaven into the Church, just as of the Church into the world. The Church is the mediatrix, irreplaceable, unique, necessary. What the Son has founded on earth is never arbitrary but always inherently consistent, deriving from dependence on, and obedience to, the Father; it subserves the necessity of bringing the world back to the Father so exclusively that, outside of that necessity, no understanding of what the Son has done for men would be possible. He bestows; and his giving is of that heavenly sphere that arches down toward men, a giving away of that which, in eternity, the Son both receives from the Father and the Spirit and gives back to them and which the world requires for its redemption.

The Son has seen the falling away from the Father, has discharged the guilt; and he completes this work by constructing a stable pathway for man's return. This does not clash with the fact that everyone, at the beginning of his quest for God, is led by grace along quite personal paths; nor with the fact that the paths of the individual always remain free within the freedom of the Lord, who reveals himself to each in unpredictable encounters. But there are also firmly structured paths of grace: the sacraments. In his encounters with individuals during his earthly life, and even more in his encounter with universal guilt on the Cross, the Lord had gained the experience that the paths of grace require such a structuring. Thus he takes over the baptism practiced by John and elevates it to his sacrament; he has himself baptized in the presence of the people, who are profoundly moved by the event: not because someone has been converted, but because the heavens open and the Spirit descends. And the people—a symbol of the coming Church—no doubt long to have something for themselves that would be similarly explicit. The Lord links up with this when he makes baptism the ineradicable sign of belonging to his Church. The Father will recognize this sign in people's souls, but no less so the traces left in them by confession, confirmation, and every other sacrament that the Son institutes.

As long as the Son was living among us, the sacraments seemed to be a gift from the Incarnate One to his fellow men, from the Bridegroom to his bride. In ascending to heaven, however, he takes their mysteries along with him, in order to enter them into that book of life which, as the Redeemer, he presents to the Father. Now, from his place in heaven, he is present within the Church in the forms of bread and wine, a presence that both demands faith and is there for it. As well, the forcefulness of his teachings and exhortations and the truth of his words have in no way been diminished. Men need only open their inner eyes and set their faith in readiness to receive the present offer of grace. Grace inheres in every sacrament in the way appropriate to each, and it also leads from one sacrament to another, so that its work can be rounded out in accordance with the requirements of each individual life. Each receives what he needs in order to live as a Christian among his fellow men and to remain true to his primary nature, which is that of having been created with a view to Christ. As a movement, this directedness of man toward Christ is just as fluid as the movement of the sacraments. And the Father observes this onward flux, recognizes in the sacraments the movement toward the Son—which begins with his creation, with bread and wine, with water and oil, with human words and human covenants, and moves on toward redemption in order to fulfill itself there. Yet this movement calls for ever-new fulfillment within the Church, in order,

through those who receive it, to pour itself forth into
the world and to set the whole of creation in movement
toward the Father. The sacraments are an invitation to
play an accompanying part in the self-surrender of the
Son, who leads the world to the Father.

From this on-flowing nature of the sacraments we
can already surmise something of the character of eternal life. We must not imagine the unchangability of
God as something static: it is the movement of all
movements, a streaming of eternity out into endless-
ness. Our earthly eye does not perceive the movement
in the sacraments; it is nothing sensible, nothing that
might visibly distinguish the genuine recipient from
the averted, the half-hearted. And yet faith is capable
of seeing things that the sensory eye does not see; for
him who can see within faith, there is a special kind of
impressiveness. And if the process is sacramental, then
it is ecclesiastical: not in the superficial, trite sense that
men find good enough for their notion of the Church,
but in one based on the bridal relationship that the
Son has entered into with the Church, that is, in a
sense that is completely recognized and fulfilled only
between those two parties. And faith has a knowledge
of this process, even if the believer is incapable of giving rational expression to it. Faith knows that it participates, without seeing, in the vision of the Lord and
that such participation is instituted in the Church in
such a way that faith itself becomes part of the Lord's
truth. And no doubt the truth of faith has so much

weight that we members of the Church, in living from this faith, can often behave in a manner suggesting that we are overburdened, that we are being required to live in a kind of "as-if" mode. But if we venture to take faith seriously, then we are at once caught up in this movement and are amazed to find that whole parts of our life in faith drift away from us: because, even now, they have their existence and fulfillment in heaven and because, through the fullness of sacramental life in the Church, they are truth even if we do not realize it, are life even if we have no idea of this, move within God even if we detect nothing of this. Thus sacramental life is something that lives above and beyond all earthly life —more powerful not only than our thought but than our being itself, because it has been included, from the very days of creation, in that impetus toward the Son which the Father has lodged in the deepest essence of all things and of man.

~

The prologue to the Gospel of John, in which the Son's eternal being is elucidated as the Word—in his relation to the Father in eternity, to the Father's creation, and to the Father's intentions for it—also describes his Incarnation and the life of the Church, insofar as the latter is represented in the Person of the Son himself.[1] The

---

[1] Cf. the author's *John*, vol. 1: *The Word Became Flesh* (San Francisco: Ignatius Press, 1994)—ED.

Son, as the Word of the Father, also wants to be the word in the Church. He desires that what he states and expresses about the Father, in the context of his devotedness to him, should also be spoken and represented in the Church, so as to be conveyed, through her, back again to the Father. Thus, in the Church, the Father recognizes and apprehends the Word that is the Son. He hears it as prayer, that is, prayer of the Son, of the Church, and of the individual members. And the three-part sound that arises from these three sources is the same one that he knows from all eternity and takes with him into all eternity: the sound of the voice of his only Son.

The sacraments seem, at first, to be bearers of a two-fold movement: first, they are the sources of a three-fold grace that descends upon men, and, second, they are the hearing of the prayers that ascend from the faithful. They are embedded in prayers, which are, in turn, embedded in the Church. The Church takes up all the individual prayers that arise within her, forms them anew, and offers them to the Father so that he might bless them and lend them a life that stems from him and that he recognizes as his own. And this recognition is, in each case, oriented toward the Son: in prayer, the Father recognizes the Son, who is the Word, just as he recognizes him in the sacraments. Thus, however, in prayer, both the descending and the ascending aspects of the sacraments coalesce to form a dynamic unity, which also reveals, above all, the unity of threefold grace.

Because of the two descents of the Spirit, at the Jordan and on Pentecost, we have grown accustomed to regard baptism and confirmation primarily as sacraments of the Holy Spirit and the Eucharist and confession primarily as sacraments of the Son. Among the latter we also include ordination to the priesthood, which is closely related to the Son. In marriage, however, many aspects of which refer back to the Old Covenant and to creation, we perhaps see the part of the Father as being predominant. But this way of viewing things is at odds with triune grace. No more than the Father can be seen as having created the world without the cooperation of the Son and the Spirit can the sacraments be individually correlated with any one Divine Person. The Father is present in all of them as the one who originally bestows everything, accompanies everything in its unfolding, and receives back everything that is accomplished. It is only we who draw boundaries everywhere, who love ready-made formulas so that we are not forced to go farther: formulas that are not false in themselves but are incomplete and, since we are sluggish, tend to impede our supplementing them. But whenever we touch on the essence of grace, we have to move beyond all boundaries until we reach the Trinity. Then we also become aware that the portion of our faith that remains deposited with God is the one that is able to grasp being as a whole, because it does not push toward reason's drawing of boundaries but surrenders itself humbly; nor has it any desire to be transplanted from its hiddenness in God into our consciousness. Humility and obedience take on a new, quite essential aspect here, which points toward the Son and his relationship to the Father. If one selects, at random, any of the mysteries in the Son's life—his birth, his concealed life, or some other—one will recognize, in contemplating it, that the grace that reveals itself there is much greater than one could have expected, that it is more encompassing, has wider effects, radiates in more directions. It is the always-more of Christ that announces itself here, the distance that separates him, as the Son of God, from everything creaturely. But it is just as much the always-more of the acceptance by the Father, the emanation of the Father's love for the Son, who fulfills all that is filial in relation to the Father. And thus there exists in every sacrament (no matter how much we think we have explained and conceptually articulated it and isolated and delimited it from the others and defined it in its very essence) a part that is perhaps much greater than the supposedly understood part: the part of the Father, which, by virtue of the Father's presence, is constantly being revitalized with a triune life that issues from the triune interchange of love.

It is clear to us that, in the process of critically assessing a famous painting, an almost incomprehensible number of viewpoints and imponderables all interact: not only the material and the ground and the forms and colors and their interplay, but also the light in which the picture is placed and the mood of the observer and the proficiency of his eye, and his memories, his expectations. And it can happen that the observer, caught up in so many secondary considerations, forgets the artist's primary intention. And yet it was there at the beginning and gave direction to everything else: from the choice of the canvas to the final brush stroke. In the same way, God the Father allows the most varied, indeed, the most disparate elements—all stemming, however, from his love—to interact in the sacraments so as to bring about the desired effect: a definite, unique effect, yet, for its countless observers, one full of nuances and infinitely differentiated. Every statement about a sacrament can be correct; none is exhaustive. The truth is a summation that is reached only in God, where it remains beyond our grasp. God alone knows it. But he does place something of the knowledge that is solely his at our disposal: every reception of a sacrament brings us closer to it, and differently closer—in the way that he wishes—if we are obedient.

An individual who prays reaches the Father with his words of prayer, because the Son is the eternal Word and assimilates our words to his. The Father hears him, and does so favorably, throughout all time. But for this to occur, an individual's prayer must be embedded in the Church's prayer. He cannot demand to be heard by

God while at the same time shutting himself off from the common prayer of the Church (which supposedly "means nothing" to him). That words of prayer have a segmental character becomes particularly clear through the sacraments: in their administration and in their reception. There, the words have an obvious participation in the dimension of the ever-greater, which, transcending everything private, attaches to the sacramental event. Of course the sacraments have their fixed contours; but there are also the shadows that they cast, the spiritual dimension in which they exist and from which they are inseparable. Just as the picture was seen to depend on its lighting, on the color of the wall on which it hangs. The setting of a sacrament, however, is always the Church as a whole, so that the individual who receives it must, in his attitude of prayer, integrate himself into that greater thing and, through this integration, himself contribute essentially to the proper setting of the sacrament. Not by his own efforts, but through grace. Thus, in turn, the sacrament appears as a nodal point of grace, that is, in its general and personal forms, which come together here. For the Father, however, these ways of grace are always interfused with the intentions of the Son; indeed, the Son responds, in the sacrament, to his own status as being the Word and thereby to that which he is within triune love.

∼

There exists in the Church a striving toward the sacramental, which also finds its expression in virginity: one of an openness toward allowing things to unfold and take effect. Inherent in sacramental life is renunciation. One can appreciate this through the example of the priest, who presides over this life and gives up much for its sake. It is a renouncing of certain thoughts, of certain acts, a renouncing of a potential developmental path that is innate in man. A renouncing of contentment in relation to another person, a "thou", who either is not encountered at all or, in the midst of an ongoing encounter, is sacrificed to the relationship with God. Something of this priestly renunciation (which is also clearly evident in monastic life) touches the life of all who participate in the sacraments. It lies in the essence of the Church herself, is the movement of the virginal Mother toward her Bridegroom—a movement that does not know itself, a slumbering self-commitment to what God wants to happen, the foundation of all forms in general, within the Church, of a believer's submission to whatever will be. The field belongs to God alone, so that he might hold sway over it as over his property. And the renunciation implicit in virginity tends toward the sacramental, insofar as every reception of a sacrament involves both an active acceptance of and an acquiescence in an effect whose depth is left to God alone, an encounter between action and contemplation in the innermost spirit of the believer. Here, physical virginity becomes a symbol of religious virginity. Accordingly, it is an opening toward God, a striving to place everything in his hands, body and soul, in a willingness devoid of all limits and calculation, even at the moment when God exerts his determining influence. This openness is not achieved with any kind of control; there is no continual reflection on what is happening; but everything is left to unfold freely in further acquiescence. As if empty spaces were breaking into each other. God the Father laid the foundation for this in the preredemption of Mary. He created her as exemplary and thus as perfect, yet still in such a way that we can take her as an example and, in looking up to her with reverence, be inspired—through her, through how God treats her and how she responds to that— to follow her. To a following that leads farther toward the following of Christ. The Mother's consent is the consent of the female disciple to whom the Lord says: Follow me. She gives it with a perfect innocence and purity that renounces any incurring of guilt, in a way that simultaneously involves both action and acquiescence. She persists obediently in her state of preredemption and presents to the Church and to every individual the example of her knowing and her not-knowing, of her remaining open and her expectation, which is ready to accommodate any fulfillment. This means that, in every fulfillment, the image of the expected is an unbroken whole, even if, in any concrete case, what was expected or promised seemed to have a quite different aspect. For the Christian, however, there remains, in the receiving of every fulfilled promise, a spirit of willingly allowing oneself to be raised to the height of what has come about and is always greater than anything expected, because it implies not just adequate but overadequate fulfillment, since the whole extent of God's elevation above man is disclosed along with it. One can say that the greater the Christian expectation, the greater the divine fulfillment; for in order to possess a greater expectation, the believer must possess a greater, more childlike, and more innocent faith —in which every space remains free for the miracle and every recognition of the divine bestowal, which takes place unexpectedly, proves itself to be precisely what had been expected, because every aspect of God's capacity for always being greater was implicit in it. Man does not, then, hold expectations in accordance with the measure of his own being but allows God to reveal himself as accords with his divine measure and the measure of what he wishes to reveal.

The foregoing example, based specifically on virginity, is at the same time valid and binding for everything sacramental, because the sacramental is always the rounding out of an incomplete expectation and affords more free space than the believer himself possesses and is able to offer. God the Father is cognizant of this; he accepts the sacramental—something dispensed to him by man within the grace that he himself dispenses—as a response to the virginity of the Mother, to her preredemption, to the Incarnation of Christ.

XI

THE FATHER AND
ETERNAL LIFE

At the time of creation, the Father was especially prominent; it was also he who walked together with the first human couple in paradise. But in all this he was accompanied, in a fully unified way, by the Son and the Spirit; there was, from the very beginning, a manifesting of the one, eternal, and living God. As soon as a man undertakes any individual act, he knows that it will not remain without an echo; it can incisively define his future life or exert some effect on others, including persons totally unknown to him and at points in time incalculable by him. And it is all the more clearly self-evident that, when God undertakes some act, especially one as significant as creation, he alone can foresee its entire consequences, indeed, that the act has the dimensions of his eternity. He does nothing without that work's having some relation to his own infinite duration. He neither excludes his creature nor rejects it. He creates it as something internal to his divine responsibility, his infinite being, his eternity. And thus man, from the moment he steps into being, is one who is moving toward God, one who stems from eternity and ends by returning to it. As a thing effected by God, as a product of God's will, he is the result of a sharing—generated by the three Persons of the eternal God—in what God is, even when, as man, he lacks all sense of this.

And God introduced a structure into created duration, separated day from night, and integrated man into this cyclical rhythm of time; and man's enduring of this process of being carried through time by God's will originally contained no question about when it might end and where it was leading. No question about the measure of his existence. God installs man as king over creation and allows him to enjoy his innate freedom. He issues only one prohibition, and this seems, in its quiet self-containedness, to have nothing to do with the length of man's existence. It simply holds good. And alongside it, everything that was allotted to man also holds good: his orientation toward God, his ruling over the world that was created for him and, without his knowledge, created with a view beyond him to Christ: so that his human time is directed from the very start toward the Son and thus, as duration, does not flow into mere indefiniteness but acquires both a directedness toward eternity and a positive anchoredness in it. Making this anchoredness known to man was not, however, part of the Creator's pleasure; he gave him the sequentiality and cyclical rhythm of time but no overview of the span of his existence.

After man sinned, his eyes were opened to that which he did not need to know, namely, the finitude of his duration; and now this end became a rupturous break, a dying. And the hour of this ever-threatening death remained indeterminable. Having thus fallen out of the security of resting within the will of God, man could reap nothing other than insecurity. And as he then begins to perform sinful acts that have no correspondence to the will of God, his actions come to share in his insecurity. Whereas he previously enjoyed a participation in divine things whose essence he did not appreciate, but which nonetheless existed for him, that participation has now been called into question. But God does not abandon his creature. The Old Testament is full of prophecies and promises that have a divine validity down through time and above and beyond time. Man seizes upon them in hope: with a view to a time that is not more precisely defined for him. And in order that he might learn once again to believe, and to open himself to divine things that he does not comprehend, the prophets are also entrusted with short-term predictions that are fulfilled within a given time and, in fact, concern things and events that seem to have been brought about through the power of the word itself: they are predicted and are suddenly there, lending an enormous present force to the divine word. They serve to recall God's power in creating the world and to impart the credibility of lastingness to his words of promise. Believers are thus able to recognize that both their lives and the life of mankind exhibit a direction, that the signs of the Redeemer's coming are increasing, and that man cannot ultimately be deprived of his destiny, for the fidelity that he failed to show toward God is shown by God toward him. It is brought before his eyes through many prophecies, and there is no scarcity of signs to indicate it. And the words of God pertain not just to the present and future but refer in each case back to the past, so that the believer always stands in the most extensive context of interrelated events. Less than ever is he excluded, since he may regard as his own such spans of time as extend far beyond him: including things that happened long ago and are reclaimed from the past by becoming meaningful to him, in his present existence, because of a significance that bears on the future. Through the word, which is realized within time—and has been realized in part, as deed and event, before his eyes—he becomes integrated into the meaningfulness that God's Word imparts to history. Already in the exit from paradise the fundamental directedness toward Christ had come to light, and man received, through that word from the past, a homeland. And that homeland in the past becomes for him, through the forward-moving word, a homeland oriented toward the future. The word has every validity; what was promised but not yet realized is on its way.

Finally, the Son appears and promises the whole of heaven. Together with him, men are to exist there where he existed from all eternity. Eternity with the

Father and the Spirit is his homeland. And now it is a matter of finding the way back not just to the origin of creation, to an act God performed in relation to time, but to God's countenance, to his most proper form of duration: to eternity. And this is already taking place now, in the era of the Church. What is involved here is not something laboriously surmised and brought to light, which would have to be pieced together, like so many individual stones in a mosaic, by reading and comparing passages from Holy Scripture, but rather, the broad interrelational patterns that are always evident in the truth of the Church, of the Son, and of the triune God. Various individuals can perhaps construe these in different ways; misunderstandings and wrong interpretations are possible. But the promises must, above and beyond everything, be fulfilled; the words of the Son will not pass away; our time will be taken back up into eternal time. And taken back up with it will be our knowledge of the triune God, the entire teaching of the incarnate Son, the truth of the Old Testament and of creation. The eternity of the Father, in which everything is to be securely contained, now appears in its incomprehensible greatness. Man could attempt a detailed listing: this belongs there, and this, and also that . . . He would never reach an end. But in every little part that belongs there, the mark that God placed upon it, which identifies it as an item of property from his eternity, can nonetheless be detected. And the whole transience of created time appears, when regarded from that perspective, as a succession of individual parts that fit together into a greater whole.

～

Under the Old Covenant, as long as the Son had not appeared, God's eternal life was opposed to, and distant from, the transient life of man. But once the Son had come, in order to bring the world back home to the Father, he wanted to accomplish that in such a way that the Father would take delight in the world for eternity and that man's delight in having once again found God would similarly extend through eternity. He therefore arranges certain "breakthrough" phenomena that are all related to one another. The Son suddenly appears amid transient time, invested with all his divinity and eternality, whose continuity suffers no break even through his death. The Father, however, reclaims him from this death as the man that he was, who has died and rises again. Thus the Father has taken his transient being up into his eternal being, his humanity up into his divinity. And with that act of taking up, something is created that can potentially be allocated to others. It remains unique but also open as such. It comes about through a dying that confers eternal life and a love that is so living as to embrace all that it encounters: all men, the entire world. And in order to facilitate the Son's work, the Father redeems the Mother of God in advance, so that she might be capable of giving birth to the infant

Redeemer. This pre-redemption is, in turn, a participation in eternal life. It is thus the eternal Virgin who conceives and bears the child. In a way that is not simply the Son's way and also not simply the sinner's way; and in a way that is so arranged, both for and through the Mother, that her word of affirmation is able to be kept without wavering. But that ability, too, is communicable and extends to the Church. It is an ability that the Mother, when she stands by the Cross, consigns to the Son so that it might be allowed to celebrate death and Resurrection in him. But it is not only an ability through the Son, and therefore not only an eternity in him, but personal eternity, a being taken up personally and bodily into the grace of eternity. A *coming to be* taken up within a *having come* to be in this state. A future that includes a past. And the future reveals what the past was, while the past—the Immaculate Conception—includes in advance the Assumption into heaven. Through this Assumption—not just as something bodily—the fact has been demonstrated for all time that the man who has not sinned possesses his homeland in God's heaven; and the promise has also been issued to all, in a manifest sign, that those who have been redeemed by the Son and cleansed of sin will return with him to the Father. The Son is the foundation of man's eternal life, but he does not want to be that apart from his Mother. Both of them are this together, in an interwoven yet differentiated way in which God's full intention comes to light. It is really *his* eternal life, which the Son has manifested and revealed to men in order to allow them to participate in it individually. The Eucharist is the prefiguration of the heavenly banquet. But in addition to it, the Son also instituted confession as a means of access to eternal life, as a casting off of the old, transient, and sinful mantle and the power to don the new, eternal, and sinless one. Thus eternal life is prefigured not only in the persons of the faithful but similarly in the sacraments of the Church. She has the task of administering these, within the word of love that was bequeathed to her by the Son. He is both: love and Word, and the Word in him is not transient; it is God. Through being taken up into the Word, which is God, the Word shows itself to those who have been taken up as the life, as the way, as the truth, but above all as the everlasting love that circles among the three Persons of the one Divinity.

Thus, by virtue of the Son's sacrifice and his having brought the world home again, the Father is able to regard men as his eternal creatures. Eternal life is not situated in heaven, far from man's grasp, something self-enclosed; it is the life-filled Word, in which men have a share because they are capable of taking it in. And that capability is itself grace; but the grace is the love of the triune God, which endures in eternity and takes up into its eternity the whole of the world that the Son has redeemed. The final, ultimately valid look of the Father is not the look that contemplates creation through the medium of his act of creation, nor is it the look of the judge who measures the extent that sinners have turned away, nor, again, the look of the just assessor who evaluates man's ever newly arising, and ever repeatedly failing, attempts at love—but rather, the look of the eternal Father, who finds in the world the consummated, eternal love of the Son.